The Best of

Ahmed Faraz

The Best of
Ahmed Faraz

Selected Ghazals and Nazms with their English Translation and in Roman Script also

Kuldip Salil

rajpal

Established 1912
100 Years of
Excellence in Publishing
rajpal

₹ 375
ISBN : 9788170289043
1th Edition : 2021, Reprint : 2025

BEST OF FARAZ
(English translation of selected Urdu poetry of Faraz Ahmed Faraz)
Selection and Translated by Kuldip Salil
Printed at G.S. Offeset, Delhi

RAJPAL & SONS
1590, Madarsa Road, Kashmere Gate, Delhi-110006
Phone : 011-23869812, 23865483, 23867791
website : www.rajpalpublishing.com
e-mail : sales@rajpalpublishing.com
www.facebook.com/rajpalandsons

Introduction

Writing about Milton, a critic says, *"Classical in art, Milton is fundamentally lyrical in inspiration. This happy synthesis is at the root of Milton's genius."* Nowhere is this synthesis more evident than in Urdu and Persian ghazal. Ghazal has a set grammar, a strict poetic form in which rules of the genre are very clearly laid down; there has to be a meter, a recurrent rhyme and a *radeef* i.e. the end line. And the inspiration of a ghazal is essentially lyrical, in which emotion perhaps has a larger role than in any other form of poetry.

Much of not only the charm and beauty of the ghazal but also its durability is due to this happy blend of the classical and the lyrical or emotional.

Ahmed Faraz, one of the greatest Pakistani poets (in fact, he is a universal poet like all great poets) is a leading practitioner of the ghazal of our times. It should, however, be quickly added that he is an equally great poet of the nazm too. The only difference is that his ghazals are better-known and are more popular.

Ahmed Faraz died only two years back (2008) on 25th August of kidney failure. His heavy husky voice still rings in our ears. He is perhaps the most sung modern poet, next only to Faiz Ahmed Faiz. In fact, after Faiz and Mohammed Iqbal, he is the greatest Urdu poet of the 20th century. Some people however like to bestow this honour on Firaq Gorakhpuri. And Firaq would have caught me by the scruff of the neck for rating anybody higher than himself.

Faraz was born in Nowshera near Kohat in North-West Frontier Province on 14th January, 1931. He comes of a respectable family of Syeds. His full name is Syed Ahmed Shah Faraz, Faraz being his pen name. Ethnically a descendent of Haji Bahadur, a famous saint of Kohat, he is the first great Urdu poet from this region. His father Agha Syed Mohmmed Shah Kohati was a well-known traditional poet.

Faraz studied at Edwards College in Peshawar and obtained Master's degree in Urdu and Persian. During his college days, Faiz Ahmed Faiz and Ali Sardar Jafri were the best known progressive Urdu poets and they impressed him the most. For sometime Ahmed Faraz taught Urdu and Persian in Peshawar. His career actually started as a script writer at Radio Pakistan. In 1976, he became the founder Director General of Radio Pakistan and later became the Chairman of Pakistan Academy of Letters.

Ahmed Faraz had started writing poetry from his student days. His father once brought him clothes on Eid. Faraz didn't like the clothes but preferred the ones meant for his brother. That led to his first foray into poetry :

लाए हैं सब के लिए कपड़े सेल से
लाए हमारे लिए कम्बल जेल से

He has brought clothes for everybody from the sale,
For me he has brought a blanket from the jail.

He was weak in mathematics and his parents sent him to learn it from a girl classmate. Instead of learning mathematics Faraz started 'Bait-bazi' a kind of couplet-recitation competition with her.

After partition of India, the poets Nasir Qasmi, Ibne-Insha and Shakeb Jalali rose to position of eminence in Pakistan. This group included Faraz as well. They were all contemporaries, having been born between 1925-1933. In his youth Faraz attended a number of Tarhi (तरही) mushairas, i.e. mushaira in which every poet recites his composition in the 'zameen', i.e. the meter, rhyme scheme, radeef, etc. of some old master. Many of Faraz's later ghazals are in the zameen of ghazals from these Tarhi mushairas including the famous ghazal beginning :

कुर्बतों में भी जुदाई के ज़माने माँगे
दिल वो ज़ालिम है कि रोने के बहाने माँगे

In the grave too, it wants to be lonely, and seeks an alibi
My merciless heart in any case wants me to cry.

As in most Urdu poets, love is the dominant theme of Faraz's poetry. It is said that he had loved a woman who left him, but the anguish of that loss stayed with him through all his life. This anguish and a sense of deprivation is present everywhere in his poetry :

इक उम्र से लज़्ज़त-ए-गिरयाँ से भी हूँ महरूम
ऐ राहते जाँ मुझको रुलाने के लिए आ

For a long time now I have not had the luxury of weeping;
Come and make me cry, O my comforter, if else for nothing.

Only a love-lorn person can write such poetry and only a very real pain of separation can elicit couplets such as :

दूर है तू तो तेरी आज परस्तिश कर लें
हम जिसे छू न सकें उसको खुदा कहते हैं

As you are away from me, you deserve to be worshipped;
He, whom we cannot touch is God to us.

Although love poetry forms a significant part of Urdu poetry, much of it is of indifferent quality. Only those couplets which have freshness about them, which either reveal some new facet of love (which is rare) or say what has often been said in a new, pleasing garb, stay :

कहा बात कर तू ऐसी, कहा इस तरह से कर तू
कि लगे नयी-नयी सी, कोई छोड़े वो असर भी

Whatever you have to say, say in such a way,
That it appears new and leaves some effect too.

Though not all of Faraz's poetry meets this criterion of novelty and significance, a big chunk does. And it is the love lyrics of latter variety which have been sung the most and have made him so popular. And this poetry is popular not only among the Urdu-knowing people, but has admirers in poetry-loving people everywhere. Many editions of his poetry have been published in Devnagari script too. One of the ghazals he is asked to recite wherever he goes, is the love lyric beginning :

सुना है लोग उसे आँख भर के देखते हैं
सो उसके शहर में कुछ दिन ठहर के देखते हैं

It is said, the people feast on her beauty.
So, let's stay in her town for a few days and see.

It is a longish ghazal on the same subject and shows some rare aspects of love, eulogizing the beauty of the beloved which gives great delight.

रुके तो गर्दिशें उसका तवाफ़ करती हैं
चले तो उसको ज़माने ठहर के देखते हैं

If she stops, the earth revolves around her only.
And if she moves, the times stand still to have their fill of her beauty.

Faraz's romantic poetry was a rage, especially among the youth, and he had a large number of female fans. In his college days when there was no mixing of boys and girls, his verses invariably reached the ladies, and it is said that there were few love letters which didn't contain one or two of Faraz's couplets. The ladies would drop their letters of admiration before him while he stood on the bus stop. Some well-to-do ones would send their missives through their servants. Once, when asked to recite a poem dedicated to women, Faraz said, "All my poetry is dedicated to women." He was lover of fine things which sweeten life.

It is for his romantic poetry, however, that some critics have labelled him as a poet of the teenager, a charge that was well answered by Nasir Qasmi and others. Faraz, Qasmi and some other friends had gone to Mecca where a grey old man learning that Faraz was in town, came madly running to meet him. He was a scholary person and was going estatic about Faraz's poetry. Seeing him, Nasir Qasmi remarked that poet who has such fans, cannot be a poet of the teenagers only.

His critics, have gone to the extent of saying that he should be grateful to singers like Mehndi Hasan, Ghulam Ali, Jagjit Singh and others for his popularity. In order to prove their point they cite a couplet alleging that 'मुझ और हम' cannot occur in the same couplet. They forget that 'हम' in the first line includes the beloved too. Such criticism is a good example of ways of the critics.

किस किस को बताएँगे जुदाई का सबब हम
तू मुझसे खफ़ा है तो ज़माने के लिए आ।

It is very difficult to explain the cause of our separation to everybody;
Come for the sake of the world if with me you are angry.

This, however, does not mean that all of Faraz's love poetry is good; it is not, and needs rigorous editing. However in a number of his lyrics, he is superb.

अबके हम बिछड़े तो शायद कभी ख़्वाबों में मिलें
जिस तरह सूखे हुए फूल किताबों में मिलें

Like withered flowers in the books, it seems
If separated this time, we might meet only in dreams.

or

ग़मे दुनिया में ग़मे-यार भी शामिल कर लो
नशा बढ़ता है शराबें जो शराबों में मिलें

Let the sorrows of the world and sorrows of love combine.
A cocktail is certainly more intoxicating than a single wine.

There is no artificiality in his poetry. Even in his simplicity, there is great charm. His poetry has both freshness and a soft touch and at times rare intensity :

वो ख़ार-ख़ार हैं शाख़े गुलाब की मानिंद
मैं ज़ख्म-ज़ख्म हूँ फिर भी गले लगाऊँ उसे

He is full of thorns, much like a rose-bough
I am a wounded all over, and embrace him even so.

or

कभी यूँ था कि हज़ार तीर, जिगर में थे तो दुखी न थे
मगर अब ये है किसी महरवां के तपाक ने भी रुला दिया।

There was a time when a thousand arrows pierced the heart, but I was not sad;
Now even the warm handshake of a friend makes me cry.

This poetry of cold passion which W.B. Yeats, the greatest English poet of the twentieth century, who had cried long and loud over his jilted love, could master only in his maturity.

Ahmed Faraz's poetry is a poetry not just of beautiful expression, colourful imagery and soft diction. It is a poetry that boldly faces and gives expression to harsh realities of life. For most of the last fifty years, Pakistan has been under military dictatorship in which there was no freedom of speech and expression, and basic human rights were ruthlessly curbed. No opposition to the ruling establishment was tolerated. Progressive writers were singled out for persecution as soon as Pakistan was created. Habib Jalib was jailed, Faiz Ahmed Faiz was hounded all his life except Bhutto's years, Ustad Daman was pursued as if he were a criminal. And Ahmed Faraz had no better luck. These writers raised their voice against exploitation, usurpation oppression and dictatorship. They felt aghast over the ever widening gulf between the small oligarchy of military rulers, bureaucracy, the maulvis and mullahas, who provided sanction to the unjust order on the one hand and vast mass of humanity, groaning under poverty and denied the basic amenities of life on the other.

In the line of progressive poets, Faraz was a poet of protest and paid a heavy price. Immediately after a mushaira in which he had condemned dictatorship, he was arrested. In 1980 he was compelled to go on "voluntary" exile to Europe and Canada. In fact a number of his poems speak of his deep anguish at having to stay away from home.

हमने जब वादी-ए-गुरबत में कदम रक्खा था
जिस तरह यादे-वतन आयी थी समझाने को
कुछ उस तरह कैफ़ियत जो आज भी है
जिस तरह कोई कहे फिर से पलट आने को

When I first stepped into the valley of my exile
Quite similar to that my state of mind is even today
Even now, I feel as I felt when I was in that alien city
Even now somebody is urging me to come back.

These were days of Zia's dictatorship, which inspired him to write some of his best poetry.

इस कदर ख़ौफ़ है इस शहर की गलियों में कि लोग
चाप सुनते हैं तो लग जाते हैं दीवार के साथ

Or

हम को उस अहद में तामीर का सौदा है जहाँ
लोग मैमार को भी चुन देते हैं दीवार के साथ

As we leave home these days, we leave behind on the shelf
Alongwith our turban, our name and self-respect.

We the crazy ones, O Faraz, have decided to build
In an age when the mason too is into the wall filled.

Faraz wrote his well known poems of protest like 'मुहासरा' (Siege) and 'देखते हैं' (We will see) in this period. According to Faraz and other progressive writers, this was the worst period for Pakistan's writers, but it provided the poets with food for thought and made protest poetry very popular in Pakistan. Here is a couplet by another poet :

जहाँ भूचाल बुनियादे-फसीलो-दर में रहते हैं
हमारा हौसला देखो, हम ऐसे घर में रहते हैं

See our courage, we live in a house;
Which harbours earthquakes in its very foundation.

In poems like 'नई मसाफ़त का अहद-नामा' (*Contract of a New Journey*) and 'ख़्वाब क्यों बेचें' (*Why should we sell our Dreams*) Faraz's affinity with common man, his love of freedom and his revolutionary zeal stand out. Every great writer upholds human values and empathises with the pain and suffering of the people. Faraz too writes a kind of manifesto for humanity.

तू सिर्फ़ रिश्ता-ए-नफ़रत ही लहराता रहा
तूने कभी दुश्मन से लिपटकर नहीं देखा

You have always been wearing your hatred on your sleeves
You have never known the joys of embracing the enemy.

Ahmed Faraz was a fearless man. Who, but he could write

पेशेवर कातिलो, तुम सिपाही नहीं...

You are professional murderers and not soldiers.

He never hesitated to speak out what others said only in whispers. He did not let adversity stray him from the path he had chosen for himself. Asked why he did not write another poem like मुहासरा, he said because in Pakistan things don't change and his poems do not get dated. Besides, he said, he did not want to repeat himself.

Although he was an admirer of Z.A. Bhutto and a member of the People's Party, it is ironical that Faraz should have been suspended from service in Bhutto's regime for writing a single line which said that books that spread hatred in the name of religion should be discarded.

Faraz like Faiz was a great admirer of Iqbal who had a super human stature in the first half of the twentieth century. From Iqbal, Faraz learnt the art of fusing the personal with the universal, as also the art of bending individual consciousness to the larger purpose of revolutionary change. Iqbal taught us to live like a poet and die like a poet.

Again, although Faraz was an admirer of other masters, especially Ghalib and Bedil, he has a very special affinity with Faiz Ahmed Faiz. Not only were the two contemporaries, they shared common ideals. Both were romantic and earthly at the same time; both were great poets of love and beauty as well as inspired by revolutionary ideals. Together they suffered persecution in Pakistan for their anti status quo, anti establishment poetry. Both were eye-sore to the ruling classes, the army rulers and religious fundamentalists, who were the pillars of support to the dictators of the day.

Faraz, steeped in classical traditon was the true inheritor of Faiz's mantle. Not only like Faiz, he was imprisoned and spent the dark days of military rule in 1980's in exile, but also like Faiz, he was loved by the people, especially the youth and nobody wrote with more intensity about love than Faraz. And while much by way of comfort and ease forsook him, his popularity never wained.

Ahmed Faraz was a great votary of India-Pak amity and peace. Like Faiz, he frequently visited India, was a special attraction at mushairas, much loved and admired by the audiences. Like Faiz again, he was popular both among the masses and elite. Some of his poems advocating Indo-Pak friendship are extremely moving, the most popular and poignant being 'दोस्ती का हाथ' (Hand of Friendship) :

दोस्ती का हाथ

गुज़र गये कई मौसम, कई रुतें बदलीं
उदास तुम भी हो यारो, उदास हम भी हैं
फक़त तुमको ही नहीं चाकदामनी का गिला
जो सच कहूँ तो दरीदा लिबास हम भी हैं

तुम्हारे आईनाखाने भी ज़ंग-आलूदा
मेरे सुराही-ओ-साग़र भी गर्द-गर्द-से हैं
तुम्हारे बाम की शम्में भी ताबनाक नहीं
मेरे फ़लक के सितारे भी ज़र्द-ज़र्द से हैं

न तुमको अपने ख़द्दो-ख़ाल ही नज़र आएँ
न मैं ये देख सकूँ जाम में भरा क्या है
न खिल सके किसी जानब मुहब्बतों के गुलाब
न शाख़े-अमन लिए फ़ाख़ता कोई आई

सितम तो ये है कि दोनों को वहम है कि बहार
अदू के ख़ून में नहाने के बाद आती है
तुम्हें यह ज़ोम महाभारत लड़ी तुमने
हमें यह फ़ख़र कि हम करबला के आदी हैं

ये हुआ है हाल इस ज़िंदगी का कि अब
तुम्हारे पाँव सलामत रहे न हाथ ही मेरे
हमारे शहरों की मजबूर बेनवा मख़लूक़
दबी हुई दुखों के हज़ार ढेरों में
अब उनकी तीरा-नसीबी चिराग़ चाहती है

तुम्हारे शहर में आया हूँ दोस्तो अबके
न शे'रो नग़्मों की महफिल न शायरी के लिए
अगर तुम्हारी अना का सवाल है तो फिर
चलो मैं हाथ बढ़ाता हूँ दोस्ती के लिए

Hand of Friendship

Many a season has gone by and many a weather
You too are sad, my friends, and so are we
Our dress, both yours and ours is equally dishevelled.
Your glass houses are rusted too
As my pots of wine are stained with dust.
The lights on your terrace lack all glow
And the stars of my firmament are merely dim-lighted.
You too know not the state of your physique
Nor can I see what is it that my wine contains
Neither has love blossomed on either side
Nor has any dove of peace come
The cruel thing is that both of us think
That the spring comes after bathing in enemy's blood
You are proud of the fact that you fought Mahabharata
And we are proud that we're used to the rigours of Karbala
Now life has reached such a stage
That helpless, voiceless masses of our towns
Buried under a pile of misery–
Their dark lives now demand light.
I have come to your city O friends, this time
Not for poetry nor for any poetic symposium
If it is a question of your ego, then
Here, I am extending my hand of friendship

Faraz advocated personal bonds over geographical boundaries.

Faraz's poem 'फ़ैज़ की याद में' (*In Memory of Faiz*) is an illustration of how some great poets revere and remember fellow poets. One is immediately reminded of Firaq Gorakhpuri remembering Josh Malihabadi, Wordsworth remembering Milton, Shelley remembering Keats and Auden remembering W.B. Yeats.

Faraz's poetic proximity with Faiz is so striking that it is sometime joked that Faraz imitated Faiz. Once at a mushaira, somebody took a swipe at Faraz by asking Faiz to recite a poem of his in the 'रंग' (flavour), of Faraz, that is which immediately reminds people of Faraz. Faiz, of course smiled and kept quiet. The two were product of the same historical ethos; they were both Marxists and were driven by the passion for emancipation and social justice.

The first volume of Faraz's poetry 'तन्हा तन्हा' (*Tanha Tanha*) was published when he was still an undergraduate student in Peshawar. It was a huge success, and Faraz has never looked back since. He won numerous awards, including Pakistan's highest civilian award, Hilal-e-Imtiaz for his literary achievements. Hilal-e-Imtiaz was bestowed upon him by the Pervez Musharraf regime in 2004. But Faraz was soon disillusioned with Musharraf's policies and returned the award. He said that his conscience would not forgive him if he remained a mute spectator in the midst of what was happening around him. "The least I can do" said Faraz, "is to let the regime know where I stand in the eyes of the people whose fundamental rights have been suppressed."

Faraz had become a cult figure in his life-time. Apart from the huge popularity of his poetry, his sharp nose, fair and ruddy complexion, great height and his intense emotional voice very soon attracted people. It is only people like Faraz, who in this age of petty compromises, sycophancy and manipulations have held their head high and stuck to the time-tested human values. They are beacons of light for all mankind. To slightly alter a couplet by Firaq Gorakhpuri :

आने वाली सदियाँ तुमको याद करेंगीं, हमअसरो
जब उनको ये पता चलेगा तुमने फ़राज़ को देखा था

The coming generations will revere you, my contemporaries.
When they come to know that you have seen Faraz.

Kuldip Salil

A personal tribute

FARAZ SAHIB

किसी और देस की ओर को
सुना है फराज़ चला गया
सभी दुख समेट के शहर के
सभी कर्ज़ उतार के शहर के

For some other country,
It is said Faraz has left taking away
All the sorrow of the city
And after clearing all it's debt

After the demise of Faiz Ahmed Faiz, the most popular revolutionary poet of Pakistan was Ahmed Faraz, who was the uncrowned king of Urdu poetry. Like Faiz Sahib, he was a darling of poetry lovers both in Pakistan and India. Faraz Sahib used to visit India almost every other month to participate in some Mushaira or a literary conference. He was always eager to avail of any opportunity to be amongst his Indian friends who were a Legion and always ready to lavish their love and affection on their favourite poet.

I had many opportunities to meet him primarily because of my son, Sudhir's friendship with him. Whenever Sudhir had a chance to visit Pakistan to participate in Lahore Book Fair or an International Publishers meet, he would not miss meeting Faraz Sahib even if it meant going to Islamabad at his invitation. Faraz Sahib and his wife played a gracious host to their Indian friends.

I simply cannot forget when Faraz Sahib very graciously agreed to have dinner at my residence and meet a select group of his admirers. He even readily agreed to recite some of his very popular ghazals at the request of his admirers. I still remember the couplet in which he talked about his creed and craft :

मेरा क़लम तो अमानत है मेरे लोगों की
मेरा क़लम तो अदालत मेरे ज़मीर की है

My pen is dedicated to my people of late
My pen is the court which would decide my fate

I, in my naivety, recited a ghazal composed by me which I later realized did not even meet the norms of a ghazal. Faraz Sahib in his magnanimity just smiled.

I would also like to recall another instance which was typical of his friendly disposition and amiable nature. Sudhir had invited Faraz Sahib and a few common friends for dinner at Habitat Center. While the dinner was on, the young crooner of the centre who had a melodious voice starting singing his very popular ghazal jaft'k gh lgh- The singer was in his elements and he really did full justice to it. After dinner, while we were moving out of the banquet hall, Faraz Sahib went out of the way to shake hands with the singer and complimented him for rendering the ghazal so melodiously.

Last time, when Faraz Sahib visited Delhi, he gave a very precious gift of a set of two cassettes of his selected ghazals sung by various renowned artists of Pakistan. This was a private recording and is something which I will keep on treasuring for my life. Every time I listen to it and I do it quite often, I am reminded of the tall towering Pathan that Faraz Sahib was ever radiating his benign smile for his friends.

As is well known, he was exiled from Pakistan for a number of years when he had to fend for himself in foreign lands like USA and UK. The story of his exile as related by him was quite dramatic. As soon as he had finished reciting a piece which was against the autocratic establishment, he was courteously asked by a Police Officer to accompany him. On reaching the police station, he said, "Faraz Sahib, I have been asked by the higher authorities to offer you two options, either imprisonment or you leave Pakistan by this evening by the earliest flight. Your ticket and visa are with me''. He was not given sufficient time to think over the choice or to get his belongings from home, when he chose to say good-bye to his own country. That was the time when there was military dictatorship in Pakistan.

Faraz Sahib had a sense of humour. Once at his residence in Islamabad when Sudhir was also there, he invited his friends for a drink saying that those who are Maulvis need not join. Let it be known that in spite of strict prohibition in Pakistan, people would find ways and means to indulge in eat, drink and be merry sessions.

Let me complete my reminiscences with an incident which happened at Delhi airport. He had brought alongwith him a few packets of books as he was at that time Chairman of the National Book Council of Pakistan. The person at the customs counter was on the point of questioning him when his superior who was standing at a distance, recognized Faraz Sahib and said, "Don't you know that he is our beloved poet as much as he is of Pakistan". Later on, the officer himself personally escorted him out of the customs counter.

Let me pay my compliments to Faraz Sahib with one of his couplets :

क्या कहें कितने मरासिम थे हमारे उसके
वह जो इक शख्स है मुँह फेर के जाने वाला

How close were we to the person
Who has now turned his back on us

Vishwanath

Contents

ग़ज़लें

नज़्में

Ghazals

अब के हम बिछड़े तो शायद कभी ख़्वाबों में मिलें
जिस तरह सूखे हुए फूल किताबों में मिलें

तू ख़ुदा है, न मेरा इश्क़ फ़रिश्तों जैसा
दोनों इंसाँ हैं तो क्यूँ इतने हिजाबों[1] में मिलें

ग़म-ए-दुनिया भी ग़म-ए-यार में शामिल कर लो
नशा बढ़ता है शराबें जो शराबों में मिलें

ढूँढ़ उजड़े हुए लोगों में वफ़ा के मोती
ये खज़ाने तुझे मुमकिन है ख़राबों[2] में मिलें।

आज हम दार पे खेंचे गए जिन बातों पर
क्या अजब कल वो ज़माने को निसाबों[3] में मिलें।

Ab ke hum bichhre to shayad kabhi khwabon mein milen
Jis tarah sookhe hue phool kitabon mein milen

Tu khuda hai, na mera ishq farishton jaisa
Dono insaan hain to kyun itne hijabon mein milen

Gham-e-duniya bhi gham-e-yaar mein shamil kar lo
Nasha badhta hai sharaben jo sharabon mein milen

Dhoondh ujre hue logon mein wafa ke moti
Ye khazane tujhe mumkin hai kharabon mein milen

Aaj hum daar pe khenche gaye jin baaton per
Kya ajab kal woh zamane ko nisabon mein milen

1. पर्दों 2. खंडहर 3. पाठ्यक्रम

Like withered flowers in the books, it seems
If separated now, we might meet only in dreams

Neither is my love like that of an angel, nor do you
partake of divinity
We are both humans, so why meet secretly?

Let the sorrows of the world and sorrows of love
combine
A cocktail is certainly more intoxicating than a
single wine,

Look for the pearls of fidelity only in the people
run aground

Only in the ruins can these treasures be found

Who knows tomorrow they may be found in the
world's syllabi—
The things for which today we are condemned
to die.

नज़र बुझी तो करिश्मे भी रोज़ो-शब के गए
कि अब तलक नहीं आए हैं लोग जबके गए

सुनेगा कौन तेरी बेवफ़ाइयों का गिला
यही है रस्मे-ज़माना तो हम भी अबके गए

मगर किसी ने हमें हमसफ़र नहीं जाना
यह और बात कि हम साथ-साथ सबके गए

अब आए हो तो यहाँ क्या है देखने के लिए
यह शहर कब से है वीराँ वह लोग कबके गए

गिरफ़्ता दिल हैं, मगर हौसला न हारा था
गिरफ़्ता दिल हैं, मगर हौसले भी अबके गए

तुम अपनी शम्ए-तमन्ना[1] *को रो रहे हो 'फ़राज़'*
इन आँधियों में तो प्यारे चिराग़ सबके गए

Nazar bujhi to karishme bhi rozo-shab ke gaye
Ki ab talak nahin aaye hain log jabke gaye

Sunega kaun teri bewafaion ka gila
Yahi hai rasme-zamana to hum bhi abke gaye

Magar kisi ne humein humsafar nahin jana
Yeh aur baat ki hum saath-saath subke gaye

Ab aaye ho to yahan kya hai dekhne ke liye
Yeh shehar kab se hai veeran woh log kabke gaye

Girafta dil hain, magar hausla na hara tha
Girafta dil hain, magar hausle bhi abke gaye

Tum apni shame-tamanna ko ro rahe ho 'Faraz'
In andhiyon mein to pyare chirag sabke gaye

---

1. इच्छा दीपक

All the sights of day and night have with our eyes
gone away
Those who had left us, have not returned till today

To whom shall we go and complain of your
unfaithfulness
If this is the way of the world, then this time you
are going to lose even us

It is a different matter though that I went along with
all and any
But nobody considered me a partner on that journey

What is there for you to see now, you have come
too late
Long since have those people gone and the town
lies desolate

We were sorrow-ridden but had not lost heart
But that courage is now a thing of the past

You are crying, O Faraz, for the twinkle of your
desire lost
Every other candle, my dear, has been blown
out in this blast

सुना है लोग उसे आँख भर के देखते हैं
सो उसके शहर में कुछ दिन ठहर के देखते हैं

सुना है दर्द की गाहक है चश्मे-नाज़[1] उसकी
सो हम भी उसकी गली से गुज़र के देखते हैं

सुना है उसको भी है शे'रो-शायरी से शगफ़[2]
सो हम भी मोजज़े[3] अपने हुनर के देखते हैं

सुना है रात उसे चाँद तकता रहता है
सितारे बामे-फ़लक[4] से उतर के देखते हैं

सुना है रात से बढ़कर हैं काकुलें उसकी
सुना है शाम को साये गुज़र के देखते हैं

→

Suna hai log use aankh bhar ke dekhte hain
So uske shehar mein kuchh din thehar ke dekhte hain

Suna hai dard ki gahak hai chashme-naaz uski
So hum bhi uski gali se guzar ke dekhte hain

Suna hai usko bhi hai shero-shayari se shagafh
So hum bhi mojaze apne hunar ke dekhte hain

Suna hai raat use chand takta rehta hai
Sitare baame-falak se utar ke dekhte hain

Suna hai raat se badhkar hain kakulen uski
Suna hai shaam ko saye guzar ke dekhte hain

---

1. दृष्टिगर्व 2. लगाव 3. चमत्कार 4. छत के आसमान

People feast on her beauty, it is said
So, let's stay for a few days in her city before we move ahead

Her eagle eye is said to be sympathetic to pain and suffering
So let's pass through her street and test the truth of this saying

It is said that she too is a lover of poetry
So let's also the efficacy of our art see

The moon is said to be gazing at her all night
And the stars descend from the skies to see the sight

Darker than the night, her tresses are said to be
It is said that dusk itself comes to feast on her beauty

→

सुना है आईना-तामिसाल[1] है जबीं[2] उसकी
जो सादा दिल हैं उसे बन सँवरके देखते हैं

सुना है उसके लबों से गुलाब जलते हैं
सो हम बहार पे इलज़ाम धर के देखते हैं

सुना है जबसे हमायल[3] हैं उसकी गर्दन में
मिज़ाज और ही लालो-गुहर[4] के देखते हैं

कहानियाँ ही सही सब मुबालग़े[5] ही सही
अगर वो ख़्वाब है ताबीर करके देखते हैं

अब इस शहर में ठहरें कि कूच कर जाएँ
'फ़राज़' आओ सितारे सफ़र के देखते हैं।

Suna hai aaina-tamisal hai jabin uski
Jo sada dil hain use ban sanwarke dekhte hain

Suna hai uske labon se gulab jalte hain
So hum bahar pe ilzaam dhar ke dekhte hain

Suna hai jabse humayal hain uski gerden mein
Mizaj aur hi lalo-guhar ke dekhte hain

Kahaniyan hi sahi sab mubalge hi sahi
Agar wo khwab hai tabeer karke dekhte hain

Ab is shehar mein theharen ki kooch kar jayen
'Faraz' aao sitare safar ke dekhte hain

---

1. दर्पण-सी 2. माथा, मस्तक 3. लिपटे हुए 4. हीरे-मोती 5. अतिरंजना

Her forehead is said to be like a mirror
So the simple-minded too do a make-up before they
see her

It is said that her lips excite roses jealousy
So let's blame the spring for it and its reaction see

From the day they deck her neck, it is said
The diamond and ruby are feeling bloated

All this may be a fairy tale, an exaggeration really
But let's turn into reality, if it is dream only

Shall we stay in her city a little longer, O Faraz, or
depart
Let's consult our stars and see what they impart

अब के रुत बदली तो खुशबू का सफ़र देखेगा कौन
ज़ख़्म फूलों की तरह महकेंगे, पर देखेगा कौन

देखना सब रक़्स-ए-बिस्मिल[1] में मगन हो जाएँगे
जिस तरफ से तीर आएगा उधर देखेगा कौन

ज़ख़्म जितने भी थे सब मंसूब क़ातिल से हुए
तेरे हाथों के निशाँ ऐ चारागर देखेगा कौन

मेरी आवाज़ों के साए मेरे बाम-ओ-दर[2] पे हैं
मेरे लफ़्ज़ों में उतरकर मेरा घर देखेगा कौन

Ab ke rut badli to khushboo ka safar dekhega kaun
Zakhm phoolon ki tarah mehkenge, per dekhega kaun

Dekhna sab raqs-e-bismil mein magan ho jayenge
Jis taraf se teer aayega udhar dekhega kaun

Zakham jitne bhi the sab mansoob qatil se hue
Tere hathon ke nishan ae charagar dekhega kaun

Meri awazon se saye mere baam-o-dar pe hain
Mere lafzon mein utarkar mera ghar dekhega kaun

→

1. घायल का नृत्य 2. छत और दरवाज़े

This time, when the season changes, who will witness
the arrival of spring
And watch the wound-like flowers blooming which
the season will bring

You will see that everybody will watch the wounds
of the injured man like a good game,
And nobody will know from where the arrow came

All the wounds will be ascribed to the murderer,
abviously
Your finger-prints, O messiah, nobody is going to see,

The echoes of my voice will be heard around my
door-step and ceiling
Nobody will care to enter my words and see the
house itself and know my feeling

→

हम चिराग़-ए-शब ही जब ठहरे तो फिर क्या सोचना
रात थी किसका मुक़द्दर और सहर देखेगा कौन

आ फ़सील-ए-शहर[1] से देखें ग़नीम-ए-शहर[2] को
शहर जलता हो तो तुझको बाम पर देखेगा कौन

हर कोई अपनी हवा में मस्त फिरता है 'फ़राज़'
शहर-ए-ना-पुरसा[3] में तेरी चश्म-ए-तर देखेगा कौन

Hum chirag-e-shab hi jab thehre to phir kya sochna
Raat thi kiska muqaddar aur sehar dekhega kaun

Aa phasil-e-shehar se dekhen ganeem-e-shehar ko
Shehar jalta ho to tujhko baam per dekhega kaun

Her koi apni hawa mein mast phirta hai 'Faraz'
Shehar-a-na-pursa mein teri chashm-e-tar dekhega kaun

---

1. शहर की दीवार 2. शहर का प्रतिद्वंद्वी 3. जिसे कोई न पूछता हो।

If we are merely the candle that burns up at night,
then the matter ends there,
Nobody will know who was fated to be in the night
and who was to see the morning fair

Come, let us from the boundary wall of the city,
city's enemies see
For, when the city is burning, who'll care to see
you on your terrace, O pretty,

Everybody is taking airs, obsessd with himself, here
Who'll in this uncaring city, O Faraz, for your wet
eyes care!

वहशतें बढ़ती गईं हिज्र के आज़ार[1] के साथ
अब तो हम बात भी करते नहीं ग़म-ख़्वार के साथ

हमने इक उम्र बसर की है ग़मे यार के साथ
मेरे दो दिन न जिए हिज्र के आज़ार के साथ

अब तो हम घर से निकलते हैं तो रख देते हैं
ताक़ पर इज़्ज़ते-सादात[2] भी दस्तार[3] के साथ

इस क़द्र खौफ़ है अब शहर की गलियों में कि लोग
चाप सुनते हैं तो लग जाते हैं दीवार के साथ

एक तो ख़्वाब लिए फिरते हो गलियों-गलियों
इस पर तकरार भी करते हो .ख़रीदार के साथ

→

Vehshaten badhti gayeen hijr ke aazaar ke saath
Ab to hum baat bhi karte nahin gham-khwar ke saath

Humne ik umra basar ki hai ghame yaar ke saath
Mere do din na jiye hijr ke aazaar ke saath

Ab to hum ghar se nikalte hain to rakh dete hain
Taaq per izzate-sadaat bhi dastaar ke saath

Is qadra khauf hai ab shehar ki galiyon mein ki log
Chap sunte hain to lag jaate hain deewar ke saath

Ek to khwab liye phirte ho galiyon-galiyon
Is per takrar bhi karte ho kharidar ke saath

---

1. दुख-कष्ट 2. सैयदों की इज़्ज़त 3. पगड़ी

My eccentricity increased further with the sorrows
of parting
Which now even with my well-wishers, I don't feel
like sharing

I have spent a lifetime suffering sorrows of separation
My friends could not surrive even day one

As we leave home these days we leave behind on
the shelf
Alongwith our turban, our name and self respect

There is such scare in the streets of the town
That the moment people hear footfalls, they shut
themselves down

In the first place you are selling your dreams from
door to door
And on top of it, you haggle with the customers for more

→

शहर का शहर ही नासेह हो तो क्या कीजिएगा
वर्ना हम रिंद[1] *तो भिड़ जाते हैं दो चार के साथ*

हमको इस शहर में तामीर[2] *का सौदा है जहाँ*
लोग मैमार[3] *को चुन देते हैं दीवार के साथ*

जो शर्फ़ हमको मिला कूचा-ए-जानाँ से 'फ़राज़'
सूए-मक़्तल[4] *भी गए हैं इसी पिंदार*[5] *के साथ*

Shehar ka shehar hi naseh ho to kya kijiyega
Varna hum rind to bhir jaate hain do char ke saath

Humko is shehar mein tamir ka sauda ha jahan
log memaar ko chun dete hain dewar ke saath

Jo sharf humko mila kucha-e-janan se 'Faraz'
Sue-maqtal bhi gaye hain isee pindar ke saath

1. शराबी 2. निर्माण 3. निर्माता 4. जहाँ हत्या की जाए 5. गर्व

If the whole town becomes a preacher what can one do
Otherwise we the profligates also can take on one or two

We, the crazy ones, O Faraz, have decided to build
In an age, when the mason too is into the wall filled

O Faraz the pride that we experienced in our beloveds lane
With the same pride to the gallows too we came

अब क्या सोचें क्या हालात थे किस कारण ये ज़हर पिया है
हमने उसके शहर को छोड़ा और आँखों को मूंद लिया है

अपना ये शेवा तो नहीं था अपने ग़म. औरों को सौंपें
खुद तो जागते या सोते हैं उसको क्यों बेख्वाब किया है

ख़लक़त की आवाज़ें भी थीं, बंद उसके दरवाज़े भी थे
फिर भी उस कूचे से गुज़रे फिर भी उसका नाम लिया है

हिज्र की रुत जांलेवा थी पर ग़लत सभी अंदाज़े निकले
ताज़ा रफ़ाक़त के मौसम तक मैं भी जिया हूँ वो भी जिया है

एक 'फ़राज़' तुम्हीं तन्हा हो जो अब तक दुख के रसिया हो
वरना अकसर दिल वालों ने दर्द का रस्ता छोड़ दिया है।

Ab kya sochen kya halaat the kis karan ye zehar diya hai
Humne uske shehar ko chhora aur ankhon ko moond liya hai

Apna ye shewa to nahin tha apne gham auron ko saupen
khud to jaagte ya sote hain usko kyon bekhwab kiya hai

Khalqat ki awazen bhi thin, band uske darwaze bhi the
Phir bhi us kuche se guzre phir bhi uska naam liya hai

Hijra ki rut jaanleva thi per galat sabhi andaze nikle
Taza rafaqat ke mausam tak main bhi jiya hun woh bhi jiya hai

Ek 'Faraz' tumhin tanha ho jo ab tak dukh ke rasiya ho
Varna aksar dil walon ne dard ka rasta chhor diya hai

I have left her town and closed my eyes on it
It is no use thinking now why taking this bitter pill
I found fit

It was never my habit to burden others with my grief
Why did I keep her awake even if I could not sleep

Her doors too were closed and people's hostility was
just the same
But whenever I passed her street I called out her name

The parting was murderous, but all our fears turned
out to be wrong
Until the new relationship, I too survived and she
was going strong

All feeling hearts, O Faraz, have for their pain found
out some pill
Only you are lonely, and go on suffering still

उसने सकूते-शब[1] में भी अपना पयाम[2] रख दिया
हिज्र की रात बाम पर माहे-तमाम[3] रख दिया

आमदे-दोस्त[4] की नवेद[5] कूए-वफ़ा[6] में गर्म थी
मैंने भी इक चिराग़ सा दिल सरे-शाम रख दिया

उसने नज़र-नज़र में ही ऐसे भले सुख़न[7] कहे
मैंने तो उसके पाँव में सारा कलाम[8] रख दिया

देखो यह मेरे ख़्वाब थे, देखो यह मेरे ज़ख्म हैं
मैंने तो सब हिसाबे-जाँ बर-सरेआम[9] रख दिया

जो भी मिला उसी का दिल हलक़ाए[10] बगोशे-यार[11] था
उसने तो सारे शहर को करके ग़ुलाम रख दिया

और 'फ़राज़' चाहिएँ कितनी मुहब्बतें तुझे
माँओं ने तेरे नाम पर बच्चों का नाम रख दिया

Usne sakute-shab mein bhi apna payam rakh diya
Hijra ki raat baam per mahe-tamam rakh diya

Aamde-dost ki naved kue-wafa mein garm thi
Maine bhi ik chirag sa dil sare-shaam rakh diya

Usne nazar-nazar mein hi aise bhale sukhan kahe
Maine to uske paon mein sara kalaam rakh diya

Dekho yeh mere khwab the, dekho yeh mere zakhm hain
Maine to sab hisabe-jaan ber-sareaam rakh diya

Jo bhi mila usee ka dil halqaye bagoshe-yaar tha
Usne to saare shehar ko karke gulam rakh diya

Aur 'Faraz' chahten kitni muhabbaten tujhe
Maaon ne tere naam per bachhon ka naam rakh diya

---

1. निधन की रात 2. संदेश 3. पूरा चाँद 4. मित्र के आने 5. निमंत्रण 6. प्रेम गली 7. वचन 8. रचना-कर्म 9. सार्वजनिक करना 10. वृत्त 11. मित्रों के आस-पास

Lighting the terrace with full moon on the night
of separation
In the silence of the night too she managed to send
her communication

The news of her arrival in the love-lane being hot,
I too lit a lamp in the evening by lighting my heart

Her eyes seemed to say something so sweet
That I placed all my poetry at her feet

These were my dreams and these are my wounds,
prithee
This is my balance sheet which anybody can see

Everybody, I met was under her spell
The whole city, it seemed, in her area of influence fell

Mothers have named their children after your name
How much more, O Faraz, do you need love and fame

वो गया तो साथ ही ले गया सभी रंग उतार के शहर का
कोई शख़्स था मेरे शहर में, किसी दूर-पार के शहर का

चलो कोई दिल तो उदास था चलो कोई आँख तो नम रही
चलो कोई दर तो खुला रहा, शबे-इन्तज़ार के शहर का

यह जो मैंने ताज़ा ग़ज़ल कही सो है नज़रे-अहले-फ़िराक़[1] की
कि न मिल सका कोई नामाबर मुझे मेरे यार के शहर का

सो मताए-जाँ को लिए हो पलट आए तेरे गिरफ़्ता दिल
किसे बेचते कि मिला नहीं कोई एतबार के शहर का

किसी और देस की ओर को सुना है 'फ़राज़' चला गया
सभी दुख समेट के शहर के, सभी क़र्ज़ उतार के शहर का

Woh gaya to saath hi le gaya sabhi rang utarke shehar ka
Koi shakhs tha mere shehar mein, kisi door-paar ke shehar ka

Chalo koi dil to udas tha chalo koi aankh to nam rahi
Chalo koi dar to khula raha, shabe-intzaar ke shehar ka

Yeh jo maine taza ghazal kahi so hai nazre-ahle-firaq ki
Ki na mil saka koi namabar mujhe mere yaar ke shehar ka

So matae-jaan ko liye ho palat aaye tere girafta dil
Kise bechte ki mila nahin koi aetbaar ke shehar ka

Kisi aur des ki ore ko suna hai 'Faraz' chala gaya
Sabhi dukh samet ke shehar ke, sabhi karz utaar ke shehar ka

○

1. जुदाईवालों

Somebody, who had come to our city from a far-off place
Has taken away with him all our city's glow and grace

Some eye, at least, was moist, some heart, at least, sad
In that city, somebody at least waited for me, at night, some door open, I had

The new ghazal I have written, is for the parted one, and to him I would like to send
But, alas, I have not found a courier to the city of my friend

The stricken one, alongwith the wealth of his heart, has come back from your city
To whom could he sell, for, he found not a single customer trustworthy

For some other country, it is said, Faraz has left
Taking away all the sorrow of the city and after clearing all its debt

क्यों न हम अहदे-रिफ़ाक़त[1] को भुलाने लग जाएँ
शायद इस ज़ख्म को भरने में ज़माने लग जाएँ

नहीं ऐसा भी कि इक उम्र की क़ुरबतों[2] के नशे
एक दो रोज़ की रंजिश से ठिकाने लग जाएँ

यही नासेह जो हमें तुझसे न मिलने को कहें
तुझको देखें तो तुझे देखने आने लग जाएँ

रब्त के सैकड़ों हीले[3] हैं, मुहब्बत न सही
हम तेरे साथ किसी और बहाने लग जाएँ

अब 'फ़राज़' आओ चलें अपने क़बीले की तरफ़
शायरी तर्क करें, बोझ उठाने लग जाएँ

Kyon na hum ahede-rifaqat ko bhulane lag jayen
Shayed is zakhm ko bharne mein zamane lag jayen

Nahin Aisa bhi ki umre ki qurbaton ke nashe
Ek do roz ki ranjish se thikane lag jayan

Yahi naseh jo humein tujhse na milne ko kahen
tujhko dekhen to tujhe dekhne aane lag jayen

Rabt ke sainkron heele hain, muhabbat na sahi
Hum tere saath kisi aur bahane lag jayen

Ab 'Faraz' Aao chalen apne qabile ki taraf
Shayari tark karen, bojh uthane lag jayen

---

1. मित्रता के समय 2. प्रेम, लगाव 3. बहाने

The wound may take a long time healing
Let's better learn to forget our old friendly feeling

A few day's estrangement cannot end
A life time's friendship, my dear friend

The same preacher, who would not allow me to
see you
If he himself were to see, he would start wooing
you too

Apart from love, there are other ways of
contact too
On some pretext or the other, I may start
meeting you

O Faraz, let's go now and join our clan
Leave poetry and become a working ma·

क़ुरबत[1] भी नहीं दिल से उतर भी नहीं जाता
वह शख़्स कोई फ़ैसला कर भी नहीं जाता

आँखें हैं कि .खाली नहीं रहती हैं लहू से
और ज़ख़्मे-जुदाई है कि भर भी नहीं जाता

वह राहते-जाँ है मगर इस दरबदरी में
ऐसा है कि अब ध्यान उधर भी नहीं जाता

हम दुहरी अज़ीयत[2] के गिरफ़्तार मुसाफ़िर
पाँवों भी हैं शल[3] शौक़े-सफ़र भी नहीं जाता

दिल को तेरी चाहत पे भरोसा भी बहुत है
और तुझ से बिछड़ जाने का डर भी नहीं जाता

पागल हुए जाते हो 'फ़राज़' उस से मिले क्या
इतनी सी .खुशी से कोई मर भी नहीं जाता

Qurbat bhi nahin dil se utar bhi nahin jaata
Woh shakhs koi faisla kar bhi nahin jaata

Aankhen hain ki khali nahin rehti hain lahoo se
Aur zakhme-judai hai ki bhar bhi nahin jaata

Woh Raahte-jaan hai magar is darbadri mein
Aisa hai ki ab dhyan udhar bhi nahin jaata

Hum duhri aziyat ke giraftar musafir
Pawon bhi hain shal shauke-safar bhi nahin jaata

Dil ko teri chahat pe bharosa bhi bahut hai
Aur tujh se bichhar jaane ka dar bhi nahin jaata

Pagal hue jaate ho 'Faraz' us se mile kya
Itni si khushi se koi mar bhi nahin jaata

---

1. प्रेम 2. [illegible]दी, कष्ट 3. पत्थर

Neither does she love me nor can I forget her and
reconcile to the situation
She doesn't allow me to come to a decision

The eyes never cease to be blood shot
And the wound of separation heals not

She is my life-blood, but in this wandering
I am hardly, if ever, about her thinking

I am a doubly cursed traveller; my feet are swollen
though
My travel-lust doesn't go

I fully trust your love, though
My fear of losing you does not go

Meeting her is a matter of joy though
But sanity demands O Faraz, don't go overboard
even so

तुरबतों[1] में भी जुदाई के ज़माने माँगे
दिल वह बेमहर[2] कि रोने के बहाने माँगे

हम न होते तो किसी और के चर्चे होते
ख़िलक़ते-शहर[3] तो कहने को फ़साने माँगे

यही दिल था कि तरसता था मरासिम[4] के लिए
अब यही तर्के-ता'ल्लुक़[5] के बहाने माँगे

अपना यह हाल कि जी हार चुके लुट भी चुके
और मोहब्बत वही अंदाज़ पुराने माँगे

ज़िंदगी हम तेरे दाग़ों से रहे शर्मिंदा
और तू है कि सदा आइनाखाने[6] माँगे

Turbaton mein bhi judai ke zamane maange
Dil woh bemehar ki rone ke bahane maange

Hum na hote to kisi aur ke charche hote
Khilaqate shehar to kehne ko fasane maange

Yahi dil tha ki tarasta tha marasim ke liye
Ab yahi tarke-talluq ke bahane maange

Apna yeh haal ki ji haar chuke loot bhi chuke
Aur mohabbat vahi andaaz purane maange

Zindagi hum tere daagon se rahe sharminda
Aur tu hai ki sada aainakhane maange

---

1. क़ब्रों 2. दयाहीन 3. शहर का स्वभाव 4. संबंध 5. संबंध-विच्छेद 6. आईने का घर

In the grave too, it wants to be lonely and seeks
an alibi
My merciless heart, in any case, wants me to cry

Somebody else would have been the talk of the
town if we were not around
The city in any case, would have a story found

This very heart would once die for a relationship's
sake
And now it wants every relationship to break

Here I am, robbed of everything with my heart lost
And this love demands from me my amours past

For the wounds you have given us, O Life, we are
with shame drowned
And you are hankering after mirrors all around

ये तफ़ावुतें[1] हैं मेरे ख़ुदा कि ये तू नहीं कोई और है
कि तू आसमान पे है तो हो, पर ज़मीन पर कोई और है

वह जो रास्ते थे वफ़ा के तो ये जो मंज़िलें हैं सज़ा की हैं
मेरा हमसफ़र कोई और था मेरा हमनशीं[2] कोई और है

मैं असीर अपने गज़ाल[3] का मैं फ़क़ीर दश्ते-विसाल[4] का
जो हरन को बाँध कर ले गया वह सुबुक्तगीन[5] कोई और है

मैं अजब मुसाफ़िर बेअमाँ[6] कि जहाँ-जहाँ भी गया वहाँ
मुझे ये लगा मेरा ख़ाकदाँ[7] ये ज़मीं नहीं कोई और है

यह जो चार दिन के नदीम हैं उन्हें क्या 'फ़राज़' कोई कहे
वो मुहब्बतें, वो शिकायतें हमें जिससे थीं कोई और है

Ye tafavuten hain mere khuda ki ye tu nahin koi aur hai
Ki tu aasmaan pe ho to ho, per zameen per koi aur hai

Voh jo raste the wafa ke to ye jo manzilen hain saza ki hain
Mera humsafar koi aur tha mera humnashin koi aur hai

Main Aseer apne gazaal ka main fakir dashte-visaal ka
Jo haran ko baandh kar le gaya voh subuktgeen koi aur hai

Main ajab musafir beamaan ki jahan-jahan bhi gaya vahan
Mujhe ye laga mera Khaqdan ye zameen nahin koi aur hai

Yeh jo char din ke nadim hain unhe kya 'Faraz' koi kahe
Voh muhabbaten,voh shikayaten humein jisse thi koi aur hai

1.भेद-भाव 2. हमारे साथ 3. मृग शावक 4. जंगल-मंगल 5. बादशाह 6. अशांत असुरक्षित 7. धरातल वाले

These are such contradictions, O God, that it seems
it is not you but someone else
You may be ruling the skies, but ruling the earth is
someone else

My journey was one of faithfulness, my destination looks
like a punishment
My fellow traveller was entirely different from my
fellow resident

I live and die for my doe and pine for union
He who caught the deer and took it away is, other
than me, someone

I am such a restless traveller that whenever I set
up my base
I realized that I should reside not there but at some
other place

Those who are my companions of just a few days
cannot understand O Faraz
That my amorous complaints are not against them
but someone who once my companion was

इस क़दर मुसलसल थीं शिद्दतें जुदाई की
आज पहली बार उससे मैंने बेवफ़ाई की

वर्ना आज तलक यूँ था ख़्वाहिशों की बारिश में
या तो टूटकर रोया या ग़ज़ल-सराई[1] की

तज दिया था कल जिनको हमने तेरी चाहत में
आज उससे मजबूरन ताज़ा आशनाई[2] की

फिर क़फ़स[3] में शोर उठा क़ैदियों का और सय्याद[4]
देखना उड़ा देगा फिर ख़बर रिहाई की

दुख हुआ जब उस दर पर कल 'फ़राज़' को देखा
लाख ऐब थे उसमें ख़ू न थी गदाई[5] की

Is qadar musalsal thin shiddaten judai ki
Aaj pehli baar usse maine bewafai ki

Varna aaj talak yun tha khwahishon ki barish mein
Ya to tootkar roya ya ghazal-sarai ki

Taj diya tha kal jinko humne teri chahat mein
Aaj usse majbooran taza aashnai ki

Phir Qafas mein shor utha qadiyon ka aur sayyad
Dekhna ura dega phir khabar rihai ki

Dukh hua jab us dar par kal 'Faraz' ko dekha
Lakh aeb the usmein khu na thi gadai ki

---

1. ग़ज़ल की प्रशंसा 2. पहचान 3 पिंजड़ों 4. जेलर 5. प्रशंसा

I was so much wracked by the sorrows of
separation
That for the first time I betrayed her faith in
frustration

Till today, otherwise, I have been longing for her so
intensely
That either I had to be writing poetry or weep bitterly

Those, whom I had deserted for your sake
Today once again their acquaintance I was
compelled to make

There is such hue and cry from the inmates of the
cage, but the hunter
Will give it out that he has released the prisoner

When I saw Faraz at her door the other day, I was
really sad
He was not known to be a beggar, however much
he was bad

उस से पहले कि बेवफ़ा हो जाएँ क्यों न ऐ दोस्त जुदा हो जाएँ
तू भी हीरे से बन गया पत्थर हम भी कल जाने क्या से क्या हो जाएँ

तू कि यक्ता[1] था बेशुमार[2] हुआ हम भी टूटें तो जाबजा[3] हो जाएँ
हम भी मजबूरियों का उज़्र[4] करें फिर कहीं और मुब्तिला[5] हो जाएँ

हम अगर मंज़िलें न बन पाए मंज़िलों तक का रास्ता हो जाएँ
देर से सोच में हैं परवाने राख हो जाएँ या हवा हो जाएँ

इश्क़ भी खेल है नसीबों का ख़ाक हो जाएँ, कीमिया' हो जाएँ
बंदगी हमने छोड़ दी है 'फ़राज़' क्या करें लोग जब ख़ुदा हो जाएँ

Us se pehle ki bewafa ho jaayen Kyon na ae dost juda ho jaayen
Tu bhi hirey se ban gaya pathar Hum bhi kal jaane kya se kya ho jaayen

Tu ki yakta tha beshumar hua Hum bhi tuten to jaabajaa ho jaayen
Hum bhi majburiyon ka uzra karen Phir kahin aur mubtila ho jaayen

Hum agar manzilen na ban paye manzilon tak ka raasta ho jaayen
Der se soch mein hain pervane raakh ho jaayen ya hawa ho jaayen

Ishq bhi khel hai nasibon ka khaaq ho jaayen, kimiya ho jaayen
Bandgi humne chhor di hai 'Faraz' Kya karen log jab khuda ho jaayen

---

1. संगृहीत 2. अनगिनत 3. इधर-उधर 4. रासायनिक प्रक्रिया में शामिल

Before we breach each other's faith in coming day
Why not, O friend, take our different ways

You too have from a diamond become a stone
And tomorrow, I also might not remain for what I
am known

You are the one and only, but seen everywhere
I too might break into pieces and float here and there

If the destination itself we cannot become
Let us be the route to that destination

The moths have long been thinking
Whether into the air or dust they should be turning

It is all in the hands of the providence
Whether love turns into dust or becomes a part of
the process

We have given up praying and worshipping, Faraz
For, the people around us have become gods

तुझको मांग रहा हूँ क़बूल कर कि न कर
ये बात तेरी-मेरी है इसे दुआ न समझ

पलट के आयेगा वो भी गयी रुतों की तरह
जो तुझसे रूठ गया है उसे जुदा न समझ

रहे-वफ़ा में कोई आख़री मक़ाम नहीं
शिकस्ता-दिल को मुहब्बत की इन्तहा न समझ

हर एक साहिबे-मंज़िल को बामुशद न जान
हर इक राहनशीं को शिकस्ता-पा न समझ

'फ़राज़', आज की दुनिया मेरे वजूद से है
मेरे सुख़न को फ़कत मेरा तज़करा न समझ

Tujhko maang raha hoon qabool kar ki na kar
Ye baat teri-meri hai ise dua na samajh

Palat ke ayega voh bhi gayee ruton ki tarah
Jo tujhse rooth gaya hai use juda na samajh

Rahe-wafa mein koi aakhri maqam nahin
Shikasta-dil ko muhabbat ki inteha na samajh

Har ek sahibe-manzil ko bamushad na jaan
Har ek rahnashin ko shikasta-pa na samajh

Faraz, aaj ki duniya mere vajood se hai
Mere sukhan ko faqat mera tazkara na samajh

I want you to be mine, you of course, may or may
not agree
It is matter between equals, don't take it as an
entreaty

Like the season past, he will come back too
He may be offended just now, he is not away from you

On the path of love, there is no final destination, honey
A setback in it, doesn't mean the end of the journey

It is not necessarily a mark of fulfilment to reach
the destination
For, those on the way cannot be called failures with
any justification

This world O Faraz, is around because I am there
My words are not just a commentary on some affair

ज़िंदगी की अब नयी राहें बना दी जाएंगी
जिस्म ढह जाएंगे, दीवारें उठा दी जाएंगी

अब मकानों में मकीं[1] होंगे न आवाज़ों के फूल
सिर्फ़ दीवारों पे तस्वीरें लगा दी जाएंगी

एक लम्हे के लिए सदियों का ख़ूं हो जाएगा
एक ख़्वाहिश के लिए उम्रें गंवा दी जाएंगी

लफ़्ज़ तरसेंगे मगर अज़्ने-सुख़न[2] छिन जाएगा
रोशनी होगी मगर आंखें बुझा दी जाएंगी

कल का सूरज हश्र वर-आगोश[3] निकलेगा 'फ़राज़'
चांद जैसी सूरतें ईंधन बना दी जाएंगी

Zindgi ki ab nai rahen bana di jayengi
Jism dheh jayenge, dewarein utha di jayengi

Ab makano mein makin honge na awazon ke phool
Sirf dewaron pe tasverein laga di jayengi

Ek lamhe ke liye sadiyon ka khoon ho jayega
Ek khwahish ke liye umrein ganva di jayengi

Lafz tarsenge magar azne-sukhan chhin jayega
Roshni hogi magar ankhen bujha di jayengi

Kal ka suraj hashra var-aagosh niklega 'Faraz'
Chand jaisi surtein indhan bana di jayengi

---

1. रहने वाले 2. बोलने की ताकत 3. गोद में क़यामत लेकर

Bodies will collapse and the walls will be broken all
around
New ways of life are now going to be found

Neither will the people be living in these houses nor
will be heard their voices sweet
Only pictures hanging from the walls will now the
visitors greet

For the sake of a moment, centuries will bleed
And lives will be lost for a single desire to feed

Words will be welling up but the power to speak will
be lost
There will be light and eyes will be switched off and
see not

Tomorrow's sun will, O Faraz, with fires of judgement
burn
And moon-like faces into ashes turn

शायद कोई ख्वाहिश रोती रहती है
मेरे अन्दर बारिश होती रहती है

Shayad koi khwahish roti rahti hai
Mere andar barish hoti rehti hai

Some desire, perhaps, keeps crying
Inside me, it is always raining

रंजिश ही सही, दिल ही दुखाने के लिए आ
आ फिर से मुझे छोड़ के जाने के लिए आ

कुछ तो मेरे पिन्दार-ए-मुहब्बत[1] का भरम रख
तू भी तो कभी मुझको मनाने के लिए आ

पहले से मरासिम[2] न सही, फिर भी कभी तो
रस्म-ओ-रह-ए-दुनिया ही निभाने के लिए आ

किस-किस को बताएँगे जुदाई का सबब हम
तू मुझसे ख़फ़ा है, तो ज़माने के लिए आ

इक उम्र से हूँ लज़्ज़त-ए-गिरिया[3] से भी महरूम
ऐ-राहत-ए-जाँ! मुझको रुलाने के लिए आ

अब तक दिल-ए-खुशफहम को तुझसे हैं उम्मीदें
ये आखिरी शम्मएँ भी बुझाने के लिए आ

Ranjish hi sahi, dil hi dukhane ke liye aa
Aa phir se mujhe chhor ke jaane ke liye aa

Kuchh to merey pindar-e-muhabbat ka bharam rakh
Tu bhi to kabhi mujhko manane ke liye aa

Pehle se marasim na sahi, phir bhi kabhi to
Rasm-o-reh-e-duniya hi nibhane ke liye aa

Kis-kis ko batayenge judai ka sabab hum
Tu mujhse khafa hai, to zamane ke liye aa

Ik umre se hoon lazzat-e-giriya se bhi mehroom
Ae-rahat-e-jaan! mujhko rulane ke liye aa

Ab tak dil-e-khushfehum ko tujhse hain umiden
Ye aakhiri shammaen bhi bhujane ke liye aa

---

1. प्रेम में स्वाभिमान 2. सम्बन्ध 3. रोना

You may be cross with me, but to hurt me, if for
nothing else, do come still
Do come to leave me at your will

Let me at least some pride in my love retain
Let you too sometime come to bring me round

Our relations may not be now as cordial as of yore
Still, let you come at least for formality's sake and
show the world that they are like they
were before

It is extremely difficult to explain the cause of our
separation to all and sundry
Come for the sake of the world, if with me you are
angry

For a long time now, I have not had the luxury of
weeping
Come and make me cry, O my comforter, if else for
nothing

I still have illusion, I still have hope from you
Come and blow out this last candle too.

वो जो आ जाते थे आंखों में सितारे लेकर
जाने किस देस गये ख़्वाब हमारे लेकर

छाओं में बैठने वाले ही तो सबसे पहले
पेड़ गिरता है तो आ जाते हैं आरे लेकर

वो जो आसूदा[1] हैं साहिल पे उन्हें क्या मालूम
अबके मौज आयी तो पलटेगी किनारे लेकर

शहर वालों को कहां याद है वो ख़्वाब-फ़रोश
फिरता रहता था जो गलियों में गुबारे लेकर

नक़दे-जाँ[2] सर्फ़[3] हुआ कोफ़्ते-हस्ती[4] में 'फ़राज़'
अब जो ज़िंदा है तो कुछ सांस उधारे लेकर

Woh jo aa jate the ankhon mein sitare lekar
Jaane kis des gaye khwab humare lekar

Chhaon mein bethne wale hi to sabse pehle
Per girta hai to aa jate hain aarey lekar

Woh jo aasuda hain sahil pe unhen kya maloom
Abke mauj aayee to paltegi kinare lekar

Shehar walon ko kahan yaad hai woh khwab-farosh
Phirta rehta tha jo galiyon mein gubare lekar

Naqde-jaan sarf hua kofte-hasti mein Faraz
Ab jo zinda hain to kuchh saans udhare lekar

---

1 आराम से 2. असली ज़िंदगी 3. खर्च 4. ज़िंदगी की मुसीबत

He, who would come with stars in his eyes shining
God knows where he has gone, taking away my
dreams along

Those who sit in its shade, are the first of all
To come with axes in hand as soon the tree falls

Those, who sit smug on the sea-shore know not
This time when the wave comes, it will go back with
the shore along

He, who would roam the city-streets, selling balloons
The people have forgotten that dream seller so soon

The valued part of life, O Faraz, has gone in life's
suffering
I am alive now only on borrowed breathing

तेरा ग़म अपनी जगह दुनिया के ग़म अपनी जगह
फिर भी अपने अहद[1] पर क़ायम हैं हम अपनी जगह

क्या करें ये दिल किसी की नासिहा[2] सुनता नहीं
आपने जो कुछ कहा ऐ मोहतरम[3] अपनी जगह

यारे-बेपरवा, कभी हमने कोई शिकवा किया
हाँ मगर इन नासपास[4] आँखों का नम अपनी जगह

महफ़िले जानां हो, मक़तल[5] हो कि मैख़ाना फ़राज़
जिस जगह जायें, बना लेते हैं हम अपनी जगह

Tera ghum apni jagah duniya ke ghum apni jagah
Phir bhi apne ahed per qayam hain hum apni jagah

Kya karen ye dil kisi ki nasiha sunta nahin
Aapne jo kuchh kaha ae mohtaram apni jagah

Yaare-beperva, kabhi humne koi shikva kiya
Haan magar in naaspaas ankhon ka num apni jagah

Mehfile jaanan ho, maqtal ho ki maikhana 'Faraz'
Jis jagah jayen, bana lete hain hum apni jagah

---

1. वादा 2. धर्म-प्रचारक 3. श्रीमान 4. अस्थिर 5. वध-स्थल

Sufferings of the world are real and so is my suffering for you
But that even then I stand by my word, is also true

What you say, O preacher, may well be true
But, sir, my heart listens to nobody, what do I do

Of your indifference, O friend, have I ever complained to you?
But in spite of me, if my eyes turn moist, what can I do

Be it the beloved's gathering, the place of execution or the tavern
I feel at home, Faraz, wherever I am

कल पुर्सशे-अहवाल[1] जो की यार ने मेरे
किस रश्क से देखा मुझे ग़मख़्वार ने मेरे

बस एक तेरा नाम छुपाने की गरज़ से
किस-किस को पुकारा दिले-बीमार ने मेरे

या गर्मी-ए-बाज़ार थी या खौफ़े-ज़िया[2] था
फिर बेच दिया मुझको ख़रीदार ने मेरे

वीरानी में बढ़कर ये बियाबां से तो फिर क्यों
शर्मिन्दा किया है दरो-दीवार ने मेरे

जब शायरी पर्दा है 'फ़राज़' अपने जुनूं का
फिर क्यों मुझे रुसवा किया अशआर ने मेरे

Kal pursashe-ahwaal jo ki yaar ne mere
Kis rashk se dekha mujhe ghumkhwar ne mere

Bus ek tera naam chhupane ki garaz se
Kis-kis ko pukara dile-bimaar ne mere

Ya garmi-e-bazar thi ya khaufe-ziya tha
Phir bech diya mujhko kharidar ne mere

Virani me badhkar ye biyaban se to phir kyon
Sharminda kiya hai daro-dewar ne mere

Jab shayari perda hai 'Faraz' Apne Junoon ka
Phir kyon mujhe rusva kiya ashaar ne mere

---

1. हाल-चाल पूछना 2. नुकसान का डर

Yesterday when my friend enquired my well-being
How ravishingly my well-wisher was towards me seeing

In order to conceal your name only
My stricken heart called out for every Tom, Dick and
Harry

Either because the market was booming or for fear
of loss in the future
My master sold me away to the very first buyer

When it was one up with the wilderness in desolation
There was no reason for my home to have feeling
of humiliation

Poetry is only a vehicle for my passion, O Faraz
My verses should not have made me feel at all small

बदन में आग है चेहरा गुलाब जैसा है
कि ज़हरे-ग़म का नशा भी शराब जैसा है

वो सामने है मगर तिश्नगी[1] नहीं जाती
क्या सितम है कि दरिया सराब[2] जैसा है

कहाँ वो क़ुर्ब[3] कि अब तो ये हाल है जैसे
तेरे फ़िराक़ का आलम भी ख़्वाब जैसा है

मगर कभी कोई देखे, कभी कोई पढ़े तो सही
दिल आइना है तो चेहरा गुलाब जैसा है

'फ़राज़' संगे-मलामत[4] से ज़ख्म-ज़ख्म सही
हमें अज़ीज़ है खाना-खराब जैसा है

Badan mein aag hai chehra gulab jaisa hai
Ki zehar-e-gum ka nasha bhi sharab jaisa hai

Woh samne hai magar tishnagi nahin jaati
Kya sitam hai ki dariya sarab jaisa hai

Kahan woh qurb ki ab to ye haal hai jaise
Tere Firaq ka aalam bhi khwab jaisa hai

Magar kabhi koi dekhe, kabhi koi padhe to sahi
Dil aaina hai to chehra gulab jaisa hai

Faraz Sange-malamat se zakhm-zakhm sahi
Humein aziz hai khana-kharab jaisa hai

1. प्यास 2. मृगतृष्णा 3. निकटता 4. निंदा के पत्थर

The face glows like a rose, the body is burning
The poison of grief can also be intoxicating

She is before my eyes, but still I thirst for her
No better than a mirage is the flowing river

Forget that union, now even parting from her doth seem
No better than a dream

The heart is like a mirror, the face like a rose, agreed
But somebody should see them at least, somebody should read

Even if with disrepute is wounded he
We love Faraz, he looks a gipsy

न अब जवाज़[1] है न मौक़ा है हाथ मलने का
हमीं को शौक रहा रास्ते बदलने का

पहुंच गये सरे-मंज़िल बखूबिए-क़िस्मत
मगर वो लुत्फ़ कहां साथ-साथ चलने का

मैं आप अपने ही पिंदार[2] के हिसार[3] में हूँ
बजुज़[4], शिकस्त कहां रास्ता निकलने का

वो साइतें[5] तो हवाओं के साथ जा भी चुकीं
नज़र में अब भी है मंज़र चिराग़ जलने का

वो सर्दमेहर सही पर गुनाहे-लुत्फ़ के बाद
'फ़राज़' देख समां बर्फ के पिघलने का

Na ab javaaz hai na mauqa hai hath malne ka
Humin ko shauq raha raste badalne ka

Pahunch gaye sare-manzil bakhubiye-qismat
Magar woh lutf kahan sath-sath chalne ka

Main aap apne hi pindar ke hisar mein hoon
Bajuz shikast kahan rasta nikalne ka

Woh saiten to hawaon ke sath ja bhi chukin
Nazar mein ab bhi hai manzar chirag jalne ka

Woh sardmehar sahi per gunahe-lutf ke baad
Faraz dekh saman burf ke pighalne ka

---

1. औचित्य 2. अहम 3. घेरा 4. सिवा 5. मौका

It is not the time to repent, nor is there any justification
For changing track, it seems, I have had a fascination

By sheer luck, I have reached my destination
But I miss very much the joys of walking with him
miss his company's fascination

I am by my own ego besieged
There is no way out for me except accepting defeat

The winds have long since blown those candles away
But their sight lingers even today

She is cold to me, but only after being generous
and kind
The sight, O Faraz, of the melting ice comes to my mind

अभी कुछ और करिश्मे ग़ज़ल के देखते हैं
फ़राज़ अब ज़रा लहजा बदलके देखते हैं

जुदाईयां तो मुक़द्दर हैं फिर भी ऐ जाने-सफ़र
कुछ और दूर ज़रा साथ चलके देखते हैं

रहे-वफ़ा में हरीफ़े-ख़िराम[1] कोई तो हो
सो अपने आप से आगे निकलके देखते हैं

ये कौन लोग हैं मौजूद तेरी महफ़िल में
जो लालचों से तुझे, मुझको जलके देखते हैं

अभी तक तो न कुंदन हुए, न राख हुए
हम अपनी आग में हर रोज़ जलके देखते हैं

बहुत दिनों से नहीं है कुछ उसकी ख़ैर-ख़बर
चलो 'फ़राज़' को, ऐ यार चलके देखते हैं

Abhi kuchh aur karishme ghazal ke dekhte hain
Faraz ab zara lehja badalke dekhte hain

Judaiyan to mukaddar hain phir bhi ae jaane-safar
Kuchh aur door zara sath chalke dekhte hain

Rahe-wafa mein harife-khiram koi to ho
So apne aap se aage nikalke dekhte hain

Ye kaun log hain maujood teri mehfil mein
Jo lalchon se tujhe, mujhko jalke dekhte hain

Abhi tak to na kundan hue, na raakh hue
Hum apni aag mein her roz jalke dekhte hain

Bahut dinon se nahin hai kuchh uski khair-khabar
Chalo Faraz ko, ae yaar chalke dekhte hain

---

1. चलने के प्रतिद्वन्द्वी

O Faraz, let's now change our tone a little
And see some more miracles of our ghazal

Parting, O love, is our destiny though
Let's walk together a little longer even so

We must have a rival on the path of fidelity
So let's outspeed ourselves, and see

Who are these people in your gathering here
They look at you greedily and jealously at me stare

In our own fire, we everyday burn
But neither into gold nor into ashes turn

We have not known his welfare for long, so we might
Visit Faraz and find out if he is alright

हर कोई दिल की हथेली में है सहरा रक्खे
किस को सैराब करे वो किसे प्यासा रक्खे

मुझको अच्छा नहीं लगता कोई हमनाम तेरा
कोई तुझसा हो तो फिर नाम भी तेरा रक्खे

उम्र भर कौन निभाता है तआल्लुक़ इतना
ऐ मेरी जान के दुश्मन, तुझे अल्ला रक्खे

दिल भी पागल है कि उस शख़्स से वाबस्ता है
जो किसी और का होने दे न अपना रक्खे

ये मुहब्बत कि फ़नाअत[1] कि इनायत[2] है फ़राज़
हम तो राज़ी हैं वो जिस हाल में जैसा रक्खे

Har koi dil ki hatheli mein hai sehra rakhe
Kis ko sairab kare woh kise pyasa rakhe

Mujhko achha nahin lagta koi humnaam tera
Koi tujhsa ho to phir naam bhi tera rakhe

Umra bhar kaun nibhata hai taalluq itna
Ae meri jaan ke dushman, tujhe alla rakhe

Dil bhi pagal hai ki us shakhs se vabasta hai
Jo kisi aur ka hone de na apna rakhe

Ye muhabbat ki fanaat ki inayat hai Faraz
Hum to razi hain woh jis haal mein jaisa rakhe

---

1. तबाही, मायूसी 2. कृपा

Everybody holds a desert in his palm, so possibly
How many can he oblige and who all keep thirsty

I don't like anybody who is your namesake
Let him first be like you and then only your name take

How many can with us even for so long go
May God bless you, my life's foe

To such a person is my crazy heart foresworn
Who would neither allow me to be anybody else's
nor make his own

Whether my love smiles on me or gives me
frustration deep
I am happy O Faraz, in whatever state he might keep

खुद को तेरे मीयार से घटकर नहीं देखा
जो छोड़ गया उसको पलटकर नहीं देखा

मेरी तरह तूने शबे-हिज्र[1] नहीं काटी
मेरी तरह उस तेग़ पे कटकर नहीं देखा

तू दशना[2]-ए-नफ़रत को ही लहराता रहा है
तूने किसी दुश्मन से लिपटकर नहीं देखा

थे कूचा-ए-जानां से परे भी कई मंज़र
दिल ने कभी इस राह से हटकर नहीं देखा

अब याद नहीं मुझको 'फ़राज़' अपना भी पैकर
जिस रोज़ से बिखरा हूँ सिमटकर नहीं देखा

Khud ko tere meeyar se ghatkar nahin dekha
Jo chhor gaya usko palatkar nahin dekha

Meri tarah tune shabe-hijra nahin kaati
Meri tarah us teg pe katkar nahin dekha

Tu dashna-e-nafrat ko hi lehrata raha hai
Tune kisi dushman se lipatkar nahin dekha

The kucha-e-jaanan se pare bhi kai manzar
Dil ne kabhi is raah se hatkar nahin dekha

Ab yaad nahin mujhko Faraz apna bhi paikar
Jis roz se bikhra hoon simatkar nahin dekha

---

1. जुदाई की रात 2. नश्तर

I have never found myself below your standard
He, who has once left me, for him I have never bothered

You have never passed nights of separation like I have done
You have never been cut into pieces by this demon

You have always been waving the sword of hatred, and really
You know not the joys of embracing the adversary

Besides my love's lane, there are other sights too
But with them, I had nothing, whatever to do

I don't remember, O Faraz, what my body looked like earlier
For, once I went into pieces, I never cared to gather myself together.

करूँ न याद, मगर किस तरह भुलाऊँ उसे
ग़ज़ल बहाना करूँ और गुनगुनाऊँ उसे

वह ख़ार-ख़ार[1] है शाख़े-गुलाब[2] की मानिंद
मैं ज़ख़्म-ज़ख़्म हूँ फिर भी गले लगाऊँ उसे

यह लोग तज़किरा[3] करते हैं अपने लोगों के
मैं कैसे बात करूँ अब कहाँ से लाऊँ उसे

वही जो दौलते-दिल है, वही जो राहते-जां
तुम्हारी बात पर ऐ नासेहो[4]! गँवाऊँ उसे

जो हम सफ़र सरे-मंज़िल[5] रहा है 'फ़राज़'
अजब नहीं है अगर याद भी न आऊँ उसे

Karoon ne yaad, magar kis tarah bhulaon use
Ghazal bahana karoon aur gungunaoon use

Woh khaar-khaar hai shakhe-gulab ki manind
Main zakhm-zakhm hoon phir bhi gale lagaoon use

Yeh log tazkira karten hain apne logon ke
Main kaise baat karoon ab kahan se laun use

Vahi jo daulate-dil hai, vahi jo raahte-jaan
Tumhari baat per ae naseho! ganvaoon use

Jo hum safar sare-manzil raha hai 'Faraz'
Ajab nahin hai agar yaad bhi na aaoon use

---

1. काँटा-काँटा 2. गुलाब की शाखा 3. वर्णन 4 सीख देने वालो 5. आख़िरी मंजिल

Alright, I'll not remember, but how do I forget him, pray
I shall hum him, through my verses anyway

He is full of thorns, much like a rose-bough
I'm wounded all over, and embrace him even so

These people talk of friends close to their heart
Where do I find him and how at all do I start

She is the source of my life, the sole possessor of
my heart
Shall I for your sake, O preacher, from her part!

He who has reached his destination travelling by
my side,
If he forgets me now I will not be surprised

शे'र किसी के हिज्र[1] में कहना हर्फ़े-विसाल[2] किसी से
हम भी क्या हैं ध्यान किसी का और सवाल किसी से

सारी मताए-हस्ती[3] अपनी ख़्वाबो-ख़्याल तो है
वह भी ख़्वाब किसी से माँगे और ख़्याल किसी से

ऐसे सादा दिल लोगों की चारागरी कैसे हो
दर्द का दरमाँ[4] और कोई हो कहना हाल किसी से

देखो एक सूरत ने दिल में कैसी जोत लगाई
कैसा सजा सजा लगता है शहरे-मलाल किसी से

तुम को ज़ोम[5] 'फ़राज़' अगर है तुम भी जतन कर देखो
आज तलक तो टूट न पाया दर्द का जाल किसी से

Sher kisi ke hijra mein kehna hurfe-visal kisi se
Hum bhi kya hain dhyan kisi ka aur sawal kisi se

Saari matae-hasti apni khwabo-khyal to hai
Woh bhi khwab kisi se maange aur khyal kisi se

Aise saada dil logon ki charagari kaise ho
Dard ka darman aur koi ho kehna haal kisi se

Dekho ek surat ne dil mein kaisi jot lagai
Kaisa saja saja lagta hai shehre-malal kisi se

Tum ko zom 'Faraz' agar hai tum bhi jatan kar dekho
Aaj talak to toot na paya dard ka jaal kisi se

---

1. जुदाई 2. मिलन के अक्षर 3. व्यक्तित्व की पूँजी 4. उपचार 5. उत्साह

I write verses for one and ask of somebody else for
union
What a strange person, I think of somebody, and
of somebody else ask the question

Dreams and ideas are all the assets that I possess
And these ideas too are borrowed from somebody and
the dreams are the dreams of somebody else

How can such simple-hearted people get well
The cure of their malady is with somebody and
somebody else their condition they tell

How a face illuminates the heart, you should see
How well-decked because of it looks the desolate city

If you are so excited, Faraz, you too may try
Nobody has so far been able to escape suffering since
the birth of the Earth and Sky

सिलसिले तोड़ गया वो सभी जाते-जाते
वर्ना इतने तो मरासिम थे कि आते-आते

शिकवा ज़ुल्मते-शब[1] *से तो कहीं बेहतर था*
अपने हिस्से की कोई शमा जलाते-जलाते

कितना आसाँ था तेरे हिज्र में मरना जानाँ
फिर भी इक उम्र लगी जान से जाते-जाते

जश्न-मक़्तल ही न बरपा हुआ वर्ना हम भी
पा-बजोलाँ[2] *ही सही नाचते-गाते जाते*

उसकी वह जाने उसे पासे-वफ़ा था कि न था
तुम 'फ़राज़' अपनी तरफ़ से तो निभाते जाते

Silsile tor gaya woh sabhi jate-jate
Verna itne to marasim the ki aate-aate

Shikva zulmte-shab se to kahin behtar tha
Apne hisse ki koi shama jalate-jalate

Kitna Aasaan tha tere hijra mein marna jaanan
Phir bhi ik umra lagi jaan se jaate-jaate

Jashn-maqtal hi na barpa hua verna hum bhi
Pa-bajolan hi sahi nachte-gaate jaate

Uski woh jaane use paase-wafa tha ki na tha
Tum 'Faraz' apni taraf se to nibhate jaate

---

1. रात का अँधेरा 2. पाँव बेड़ियों में

He broke all bonds as he left from here
There were ties enough, otherwise, to visit each other

Rather than cribbing about the darkness of the night
We should have lit a candle and made some
contribution to light

How easy it was, dear, in your separation to die
But it took a lifetime for the death to come by

Executions were not carried out, otherwise even though
we are in fetters
Dancing and singing we would have gone there

It is for him to say whether he was faithful or not
But, Faraz, at least you should have properly done
you part

अगर किसी से मरासिम[1] बढ़ाने लगते हैं
तेरे फ़िराक़ के दुःख याद आने लगते हैं।

हमें सितम का गिला क्या, कि ये जहाँ वाले
कभी-कभी तेरा दिल भी दुखाने लगते हैं।

पलक झपकते ही दुनिया उजाड़ देती है
वो बस्तियाँ जिन्हें बसते ज़माने लगते हैं।

'फ़राज़' मिलते हैं ग़म भी नसीब वालों को
हर इक के हाथ कहाँ ये ख़ज़ाने लगते हैं।

Agar kisi se marasim badhane lagte hain
Tere firaq ke dukh yaad aane lagte hain

Humein sitam ka gila kya, ki ye jahan wale
Kabhi-kabhi tera dil bhi dukhane lagte hain

Palak jhapakte hi duniya ujaar deti hai
Woh bastiyan jinhen baste zamane lagte hain

'Faraz' milte hain ghum bhi naseeb walon ko
Her ek ke hath kahan ye khazane lagte hain

---

1. संबंध

If I ever think of forming a relationship new
I am immediately reminded of what I had to suffer
when I had to be away from you

I don't care what injustice to me these people do
But I do mind when they start being unfair to you

That which take centuries to create
In no time do the folks here decimate

These sorrows too are a lucky man's lot
Everybody, O Faraz, gets them not

दिल गिरफ़्ता ही सही बज़्म[1] सजा ली जाए
यादे-जानाँ से कोई शाम न .खाली जाए

रफ़्ता-रफ़्ता यही ज़िंदाँ में बदल जाते हैं
अब किसी शहर की बुनियाद न डाली जाए

वह मरव्वत[2] से मिला है तो झुका दूँ गर्दन
मेरे दुश्मन का कोई वार न .खाली जाए

बेनवा[3] शहर का साया है मेरे दिल पे 'फ़राज़'
किस तरह से मेरी आशुफ़्ता-ख़्याली[4] जाए

Dil girafta hi sahi bazm saja li jaye
Yaade-jaanan se koi shaam na khali jaye

Rafta-rafta yahi zindan mein badal jaate hain
Ab kisi shehar ki buniyad na dali jaye

Woh maravvat se mila hai to jhuka dun gardan
Mere dushman ka koi vaar na khali jaye

Benava shehar ka saya hai mere dil pe 'Faraz'
Kis tarah se meri aashufta-khyali jaye

---

1. गोष्ठी 2. शिष्टता 3. बेवफ़ा 4. मिथ्या-विचार

We may be sad, but the gathering must be held
Not an evening should go without remembering
the beloved

Gradually it is bound to turn into a big prison
Better it is, not to lay any town's foundation

As he has met me with affection, my head before
him is bowed
Let my enemy now freely put me to sword

I am under the shadow, O Faraz, of a dead city
How can I possibly from uneasy thoughts be free

शामे-शबे-फ़िराक़ है दिले नामुराद संभल के रो
ये किसी की बज़्मे-निशात[1] है यहाँ क़तरा क़तरा पिघल के रो

कोई आशना[2] हो कि ग़ैर हो न किसी से हाल बयान कर
ये कठोर लोगों का शहर है कहीं दूर-पार निकल के रो

किसे क्या पड़ी सरे-अंजुमन कि सुने तेरी कहानियां
जहाँ कोई तुझसे बिछड़ गया उसी राहगुज़र पे चलके रो

यहाँ और भी हैं गिरफ़्त-दिल[3], कभी अपने जैसों से जाके मिल
तेरे दुख से बढ़के हैं जिनके दुख कभी उनकी आग में जलके रो

ग़मे हिज्र लाख कड़ा सही, तू 'फ़राज़' कुछ तो ख़्याल कर
मेरी जाँ, ये महफ़िले-शे'र है, सो न साथ-साथ ग़ज़ल के रो

Shame-shabbe firaq hai diley namurad sambhal ke ro
Ye kisi ki bazme-nishat hai yahan qatra qatra pighal ke ro

Koi aashna ho ki ghair ho na kisi se haal bayan kar
Ye kathor logon ka shehar hai kahin door-paar nikal ke ro

Kise kya pari sare-anjuman ki sune teri kahaniyan
Jahan koi tujhse bichhar gaya usee raahguzar pe chalke ro

Yahan aur bhi hain giraft-dil, kabhi apne jaison se jaake mil
Tere dukh se badhke hain jinke dukh kabhi unki aag mein jalke ro

Ghum-e-hijra lakh kara sahi, tu Faraz kuchh to khyal kar
Meri Jaan, ye mehfile-sher hai, so na sath-sath gazal ke ro

---

1. खुशी की महफ़िल 2. परिचित 3. दुखी दिल वाले

Like the candle on the night of parting, O my wretched heart weep carefully
It is somebody's joyous gathering, melt bit by bit and cry quietly

Be it a stranger or a friend, open not your heart before anybody
Go far away from here and cry, for, this is a hard-hearted city

Why should anybody bother to hear your tale in this assembly
Go and cry at a place where you were separated from somebody

There are other grief stricken people go sometime and meet them too
Burn in their fire and cry for those who are suffering more than you

The grief of parting, dear Faraz, may well be unbearable
This is a poet's gathering, so don't cry as you recite your ghazal

जुज़[1] तेरे कोई भी दिन रात न जाने मेरे
तू कहाँ है मगर ऐ दोस्त पुराने मेरे

तू भी खुशबू है मगर मेरा तजस्सुस[2] बेकार
बर्गे-आवारा[3] की मानिंद[4] ठिकाने मेरे

शमा की लौ थी कि वह तू था मगर हिज्र[5] की रात
देर तक रोता रहा कोई सिरहाने मेरे

ख़ल्क़[6] की बेख़बरी है कि मेरी रुसवाई
लोग मुझ को ही सुनाते हैं फ़साने मेरे

लुट के भी खुश हूँ कि अश्कों[7] से भरा है दामन
देख ग़ारत-गर[8] दिल ये भी ख़ज़ाने मेरे

आज इक और बरस बीत गया उसके बग़ैर
जिसके होते हुए होते थे ज़माने मेरे

Juz tere koi bhi din raat na jane mere
Tu kahan hai magar ae dost purane mere

Tu bhi khshboo hai magar mera tajassus bekar
Barge-awara ki manind thinkane mere

Shama ki lau thi ki voh tu tha magar hijra ki raat
Der tak rota raha koi sirhane mere

Khalq ki bekhabri hai ki meri ruswai
Log mujh ko hi sunate hain fasane mere

Lut ke bhi khush hoon ki ashkon se bhara hai daman
Dekh ghaarat-gar dil ye bhi khazane mere

Aaj ik aur baras beet gaya uske bagair
Jiske hote hue hote the zamane mere

---

1. विना 2. जिज्ञासा 3. आवारा पत्ते 4. भाँति 5. जुदाई 6. प्रकृति 7. आँसू 8. विनाशक

Nobody except you can my state comprehend
Where have you disappeared, O my good old friend

You are like the fragrance though, don't be for me searching
My abodes are like the lightning, fleeting

Whether it was the light of the candle or you, but on the night of parting
For long, it was by my bedside weeping

Is it ignorance of the people, or is it for my ill-fame
To tell me my story the people came

Even when ruined, O heart, I am glad that I have wealth of tears
O my destroyer, here you see my treasures

He, because of whom I could call the world my own
Without him now a full one year is gone

चलो कि कूचा-ए-दिलदार चलके देखते हैं
किसे-किसे है ये आज़ार, चलके देखते हैं

सुना है ऐसा मसीहा कहीं से आया है
कि उसको शहर के बीमार चलके देखते हैं

हम अपने बुत को, ज़ुलेखा लिये है यूसुफ़ को
है कौन रौनक़े-बाज़ार चलके देखते हैं

सुना है दैरो-हरम[1] में तो वो नहीं मिलता
सो अबके उसको सरे-दार[2] चलके देखते हैं

'फ़राज़' असीर[3] है उसका कि वो फ़राज़ का है
है कौन किसका गिरफ़्तार, चलके देखते हैं

Chalo ki kucha-e-dildar chalke dekhte hain
Kise-kise hai ye aazaar, chalke dekhte hain

Suna hai aisa masiha kahin se aaya hai
Ki usko shehar ke bimaar chalke dekhte hain

Hum apne but ko, Zulekha liye hai Yusuf ko
Hai kaun raunaq-e-bazar chalke dekhte hain

Suna hai dairo-harm mein to woh nahin milta
So abke usko sare-daar chalke dekhte hain

'Faraz' aseer hai uska ki woh Faraz ka hai
Hai kaun kiska giraftar, chalke dekhte hain

---

1. मन्दिर-मस्जिद 2. फांसी का तख्ता 3. प्रभावाधीन, गुलाम

Let us go to the lovers street and see
Who all are so stricken with love as we

Such a physician is said to be visiting the city
That the patients walk all the way to see him

While Zulekha goes with her Yusuf, we go carrying
our body
Who attracts more notice in the market, let us see

He is found neither in temple nor in a mosque, we hear
So let us visit the gallows and see if he is there

Whether he is enthralled by Faraz, or Faraz is under
his spell
Who is enthralled by whom, let us first see and then tell

Nazms

क़लम सुर्ख़रू है

क़लम सर्ख़रू है
कि जो उसने लिखा
वही आज मैं हूं
वही आज तू है
क़लम ने लिखा था
कि जब भी ज़बानों पे पहरे लगे हैं
तो बाज़ू सनाँ[1] तोलते हैं
कि जब भी लबों पर ख़मोशी के ताले पड़े हों
तो ज़िन्दा के दीवारों-दर बोलते हैं
कि जब हर्फ़ ज़ंजीर होता है
शमशीर[2] होता है आख़िर
तो आमिर[3] की तक़दीर होता है आख़िर
कि जो हर्फ़ है ज़ीस्त[4] की आबरू[5] है
क़लम सुर्ख़रू है

→

Qalam surkhru hai
Ki jo usne likha
Vahi aaj main hoon
Vahi aaj tu hai
Qalam ne likha tha
Ki jab bhi zabanon pe pehre lage hain
To bazoo sanaan tolte hain
Ki jab bhi labon par khamoshi ke tale pare hon
To zindan ke deewarodar bolte hain
Ki jab hurf zanjir hota hai
Shamsheer hota hai aakhir
To aamir ki taqdir hota hai aakhir
Ki jo hurf hai zeest ki aabru hai
Qalam surkharu hai

---

1. भाला 2. तलवार 3. शासक 4. जीवन 5. इज़्ज़त, लाज

The pen is satisfied

The pen is satisfied
That I am today what it writes
And so are you.
The pen had written :
Whenever the tongues are tied
The arms become spears
Whenever the lips are sealed
The walls of the prison house cry out,
Whenever the word is chained
It becomes a sword
And seals the fate of the tyrant—
Word is the essence of life ;
The pen is satisfied

→

क़लम ने लिखा था
ये धरती उसी की है जो
ज़ुल्म के मौसमों में
खुले आसमानों तले
उसकी मिट्टी में अपना लहू घोलता है
जो अपने लहू की तमाज़त[1] से
ज़ुल्फ़े-नुमू[2] की गिरह खोलता है
वही जिसकी पोरों के मस से
सकूते-ज़मीं बोलता है
मगर जिसने बोया था काटा था
उसके मुक़द्दर में नाने-जवीं[3] तक न थी
जिसका पैकर मशक़्क़त से पथरा गया
और जिसके लबों पर नहीं तक न थी
उसी से इबारत[4] ये सब रंगो-बू है
क़लम सुर्ख़रू है

→

Qalam ne likha tha
Ye dharti usee ki hai jo
Zulm ke mausamon mein
Khule aasmaanon tale
Uski mitti mein apna lahu gholta hai
Jo apne lahu ki tamazat se
Zulfe-numu ki girah kholta hai
Vahi jiski poron ke mas se
Sakute-zamin bolta hai
Magar jisne boya tha kaata tha
Uske muqaddar mein naane-javin tak na thi
Usee se ibarat ye sab rango-bu hai
Qalam surkharu hai

---

1. गर्मी 2. बढ़ना, विकसित होना 3. मोटी रोटी, ज्वार की रोटी 4. लिखी हुई, के लिए

The pen had written
The earth belongs to him
Who in this age of tyranny
Irrigates it with his blood,
Who with the blood of his heart
Unlocks new vistas of progress
Whose very touch
Makes the silent earth speak
He who had sown the seeds and harested the crop
But in return, got not even coarse bread
And demurred not—
All the colour and fragrance
Is because of him and is his by right
The pen is satisfied

→

क़लम सुर्ख़रू है
कि उसने लिखा था
वो बाज़ू
जो पत्थर से हीरे तराशें
मगर बे-निशाँ उनके घर
बे कफ़न उनकी लाशें
वही कोहकन
जिनके तेशे[1] पहाड़ों के दिल चीर डालें
मगर ख़ुसरवाने-जहाँ उनकी शीरीं चुरा लें
वही जिनके जिस्मों के पैवंद
अहले-हवस की क़बा में लगे थे
वही सादा दिल
जिनकी नज़रें फ़लक पर जमीं थीं
तो लब मुनइमों[2] की सना में लगे थे
अब उनकी सना चार सू है
क़लम सुर्ख़रू है

Qalam surkharu hai
Ki usne likha tha
Voh baazu
Jo pathar se heere tarashen
Magar be-nishan unke ghar
Be kafan unki lashen
Vahi kohkan
Jinke teshe paharon ke dil cheer dalen
Magar khusarwane-jahan unki shireen chura len
Vahi jinke jismon ke paivand
Ahle-havas ki qaba mein lage the
Vahi saada dil
Jinki nazrein falak per jamin thin
To lab munaimon ki sana mein lage the
Ab unki sana char su hai
Qalam surkhru hai

---

1. कुदाल 2. नेमत देने वाला मालदार

The pen had written
Those who carve out diamonds from stones
But live anonymous
And whose dead bodies do not get even coffin,
Those who hew the hearts of stony mountains
with their picks
But whose loved ones are stolen away
By the monsters of the earth,
Those, the patches of whose skin
Are woven into the gowns of the exploiters—
Those simple-hearted people
Who stared at the skies
And sang glories to the rich
They will be praised everywhere—
The pen is victorious.

चलो उस बुत को भी रो लें

चलो उस बुत को भी रो लें
जिसे सबने कहा पत्थर
मगर हमने ख़ुदा समझा
ख़ुदा समझा
कि हमने पत्थरों में उम्र काटी थी
कि हमने माअबदों[1] की ख़ाक चाटी थी
कि पत्थर तो कहीं दीवारे-ज़िन्दाँ
और कहीं दहलीज़े-मक़तल थे
कभी सरमाय-ए-दामाने-ख़िल्क़त[2]
और कभी बख़्ते-जुनूँ केशाँ[3]
कभी उनका हदफ़[4] दूकाने-शीशागर[5]
कभी सूरत-गरे[6]-हंगाम-ए-तिफ्लाँ[7]
कभी बेनूर[8] आँखों के निशाँ
बे-अश्क बे-अरमाँ
कभी लौहे-मज़ारे[9]-जाँ

Chalo us but ko bhi ro len →
Jise sabne kaha patthar
Magar humne khuda samjha
Khuda samjha
Ki humne pattharon mein umra kaati thi
Ki humne maabadon ki khaaq chaati thi
Ki patthar to kahin deeware-zindan
Aur kahin dehlize-maqtal the
Kabhi sarmay-e-damane-khilqat
Aur kabhi bakhte-junoon keshan
Kabhi unka hadaf dukan-e-shishagar
Kabhi surat-gare-hangam-e-tiflan
Kabhi benoor aankhon ke nishaan
Be-ashq be-armaan
Kabhi lauhe-mazare-jaan

---

1. पूजा स्थल 2. जनता के दामन की पूंजी 3. दीवानों का भाग्य 4. निशाना 5. शीशा बनाने वालों की दुकान 6. मूर्ति बनाने वाला, की तरह 7. बच्चों का हंगामा 8. प्रकाशहीन 9. मज़ार पर लिखी जाने वाली तख़्ती

Let us mourn her also

Let us also mourn that idol
Whom everybody considered a stone
But whom I regarded as God
Because all my life I had spent among stones
And moved from one place of worship to another
I met stones sometimes as prison walls
Sometimes, as school thresholds,
Sometimes, I saw that stones were the only thing
That masses had as their capital
Or a passionate, dedicated soul had received,
Sometimes, stones were the only remnant
Of the glass-maker's shop
Or of the sculptor of naughty children;
Sometimes, I met stones in the
form of sightless eyes
Or as the hope of one who would not cry,
And sometimes as slabs of the grave.

→

न चारागर न अहले-दर्द के दरमाँ
मगर वो बुत
चराग़े-बज़्मे-तन्हाई
मुजस्सम रंगो-रअनाई[1]
फ़ज़ा की रौशनी
आँखों की बीनाई[2]
सुकूने-जाँ
वो आँखें दर्द की झीलें
वो लब चाहत के शोलों से भरे मरजाँ[3]
वो बुत-इन्साँ
मगर हमने वफ़ूरे-शौक़[4] *में*
फ़र्ते-अक़ीदत[5] *से कहा यज़दाँ*[6]
ये हम काफ़िर
कि दुनिया कम-नज़र नादाँ
सभी लाए हमारे सामने औराक़े-पारीना[7]

Na charagar na ahle-dard ke darmaan →
Magar woh but
Charaghe-bazme-tanhai
Mujassam rango-ranaai
Faza ki raushni
Aankhon ki binaai
Sukune-jaan
Woh aankhen dard ki jhilen
Woh lab chahat ke sholon se bhare marjaan
Woh but-insaan
Magar humne vafure-shauq mein
Farte-aqidat se kaha yazdan
Ye hum kafir
Ki duniya kam-nazar nadaan
Sabhi laye humare samne auraqe-pareena

---

1. पूरी तरह से सौन्दर्य की मूर्ति 2. दृष्टि 3. मोती 4. इश्क़ का जोश 5. आस्था के जोश 6. भगवान 7. पुराने पन्ने

These stones had no sympathy, no cure for pain
But these stones were the only colour,
The only light in my loneliness
An embodiment of joy
A glow and the sight of my eyes.
Her eyes brimming with anguish
Gave me solace supreme
And those pearly lips were seductive indeed
She was human
But because of my excessive love,
Because of my worshipful bent of mind
I regarded her god,
I was an infidel
An unworldly fool.
People showed me pages of old tales

→

कि जिन पर नक़्श थे
अहले-वफ़ा के अक्से-दैरीना[1]
शिकस्ता इस्तख़्वाँ[2] *बेजान नाबीना*[3]
जबीं सजदों से दाग़ी
और ज़ख़्मों से भरा सीना, और उनके बुत
मआले-सोज़े-अहले-दिल[4] *से बेपरवा*
सभी ख़ुद बीनो-ख़ुद-आरा[5]
हर एक महफ़िल-नशीं[6] *तन्हा*
मगर मसरूफ़े-नज़ारा।
और अब हम भी गिरफ़्त दिल[7]
न महरूमी को सह पाएँ
न बर्बादी छिपाने के रहे क़ाबिल

→

Ki jin per naksh the
Ahle-wafa ke akse-daireena
Shikasta istkhwan bejaan nabeena
Jabeen sajdon se daagi
Aur zakhmon se bhara seena, aur unke but
Maale-soze-ahle-dil se beparva
Sabhi khud beeno-khud-aara
Har ek mehfil-nashin tanha
Magar masrufe-nazzara
Aur ab hum bhi giraft dil
Na mehrumi ko seh paen
na barbadi chhipane ke rahe kabil

---

1 पुरानी तस्वीरें 2 टूटी हड्डियाँ 3. नेत्रहीन 4. दिल वाले के दर्द के नतीजे 5. स्वयं को देखने सजाने वाला 6. पर्दा करने वाली औरत 7. उदास।

On which were printed the stories of true lovers :
Lifeless and wounded
With bones broken
And foreheads bearing marks of rubbing
on the beloved's thresholds,
And their beloved cold and indifferent to
the anguish and agony of those lovers,
Utterly smug and self-centred
And now sad and broken-hearted,
Neither can I bear the loss nor hide my ruination.
She is a stone slab

→

वो बुत मरमर की सिल[1]
और अहले-सजदा की जबीं घायल
सभी की बात सच
और हम नदामत के अर्क़ में तरबतर
शर्मिन्दगी के कर्ब से बिस्मिल[2]
चलो अब अपने जैसे नामुरादों से हँसें बोलें
जो वो कहते हैं वो हो लें
जबीं के दाग़ आँखों का लहू धो लें
चलो उस बुत को भी रो लें

Voh but marmer ki sil
Aur ahle-sajda ki jabeen ghayal
Sabhi ki baat sach
Aur hum nadamat ke arq mein tarbatar
Sharmindgi ke karb se bismil
Chalo ab apne jaise namuradon se hansen bolen
Jo woh kehte hain woh ho len
Jabin ke daag aankhon ka lahu dho len
Chalo us but ko bhi ro len

---

1. पत्थर की पट्टी 2. घायल

And my forehead wounded from rubbing.
People were right
And I am bowed down with regret and shame
Let me go now, and join the company of failures
like me
And do as they do
And wash the blood from my eyes and
the mark from my forehead
Let me now mourn her too.

वापसी

उसने कहा
सुनो
अहद[1] निभाने की ख़ातिर मत आ
अहद निभाने वाले अक्सर
मजबूरी या महजूरी[2] की थकन से लौटा करते हैं
तुम जाओ
और दरिया-दरिया प्यास बुझाओ
जिन आँखों में डूबो
जिस दिल में भी उतरो
मेरी जलन आवाज़ न देगी
लेकिन जब मेरी चाहत
और मेरी ख़्वाहिश की लौ
इतनी तेज़ और इतनी
ऊँची हो जाए
जब दिल रो दे
तब लौट आना

Usne kaha
Sun
Ahad nibhane ki khatir mat aa
Ahad nibhane wale aksar
Majburi ya mehjuri ki thakan se lauta karte hain
Tum jao
Aur dariya-dariya pyas bujhao
Jin aankhon mein dubo
Jis dil mein bhi utro
Meri jalan awaz na degi
Lekin jab meri chahat
Aur meri khwahish ki lau
Itnee tez aur itnee
Unchi ho jaye
Jab dil ro de
Tab laut aana

---

1. वचन 2. जुदाई

Return

'Listen', she said
'Do not come back merely to keep your word;
For, such people return
Only when they are helpless or can no
longer bear separation.
Go, and drink at every stream
Drown in anybody's eyes, you like
And sink in any heart,
I will just not feel jealous.
But when the flame of your desire for me
Burns so bright, becomes so high
That you cry
Then, you may return.

हवाओं की बशारत[1]

तमाम माँओं के होंट पत्थर हैं
और आँखों में ज़ख़्म हैं
और दिल तपते हैं
रात कहती है
उनके बेटों को
शब[2] *गए*
चंद लशकरी[3]
साथ ले गए थे
तो अब तलक उनकी वापसी की ख़बर नहीं है
न वापसी का गुमान रखना
हवायें सहमे हुये चराग़ों से कह गईं थीं
कि आने वाली रुतों के आग़ाज़[4] *तक*
तुम्हारे नसीब में रोशनी का कोई सफ़र नहीं है
ये माँएं पत्थर बनी रहेंगी
और उनके आँसू जमे रहेंगे
और उनकी आहें थमी रहेंगी
न जी सकेंगी, न मर सकेंगी

Tamam maaon ke hont pathar hain
Aur aankhon mein zakhm hain
Aur dil tapakte hain
Raat kehti hai
Unke beton to
Shab gaye
Chand lashkari
Sath le gaye the
To ab talak unki vapsi ki khabar nahin hai
Na vapsi ka guman rakhna
Hawaen sehme hue charagon se keh gain thin
Ki aane wali ruton ke aagaaz tak
Tumhare naseeb mein roshni ka koi safar nahin hai
Ye maayen pathar bani rahengi
Aur unke aansu jame rahenge
Aur unki aahen thami rahengi
Na ji sakengi, na mar sakengi

---

1. खुशखबरी 2. रात 3. सैनिक 4. आरंभ

Tiding from the Winds

Stone-silent are the lips of their mothers,
Their hearts burn
And the eyes are swollen—
The report is, that late last night
The soldiers have taken away their sons
And so far
There is no inkling of their return.
The winds had told the waiting candles
"Don't expect them to come back
Till the onset of new season;
Till then
You are destined to be lightless,
Till then their mothers
Will remain images of stone
Their tears will remain frozen
And their breath suspended.
They would neither be dead nor living
Till then."

दोस्ती का हाथ

गुज़र गये कई मौसम, कई रुतें बदलीं
उदास तुम भी हो यारो, उदास हम भी हैं
फक़त तुमको ही नहीं चाकदामनी का गिला
जो सच कहूँ तो दरीदा लिबास हम भी हैं
तुम्हारे आइनाखाने भी ज़ंग-आलूदा
मेरे सुराही-ओ-सागर भी गर्द-गर्द-से हैं
तुम्हारे बाम की शम्में भी ताबनाक नहीं
मेरे फ़ल्क के सितारे भी ज़र्द-ज़र्द से हैं
न तुमको अपने ख़द्दों-खाल ही नज़र आयें
न मैं ये देख सकूं जाम में भरा क्या है
न खिल सके किसी जानब मुहब्बतों के गुलाब
न शाख़े-अमन लिये फ़ाख़ता कोई आई

→

Guzar gaye kai mausam, kai ruten badlin
Udas tum bhi ho yaro, udas hum bhi hain
Faqat tumko hi nahin chaakdamani ka gila
Jo sach kahun to darida libaas hum bhi hain
Tumhare aainakhane bhi zang-aaluda
Mere surahi-o-sagar bhi gard-gard-se- hain
Tumhare baam ki shammein bhi taabnaak nahin
Mere falak ke sitare bhi zard-zard se hain
Na tumko apne khaddon-khal hi nazar aayen
Na main ye dekh sakun jaam mein bhara kya hai
Na khil sake kisee janab muhabbaton ke gulab
Na shakhe-aman liye fakhta koi aai

Hand of Friendship

Many a season has gone by and many a weather
You too are sad, my friends, and so are we
Our dress, both yours and mine, is equally dishevelled;
Rusted, all rusted are your glass houses
As my pots of wine are stained with dust
The lights on your terrace lack all glow
And the stars of my firmament are merely dim-lighted,
You too know not the state of your mind and body
Nor can I see what my wine contains;
Neither has love blossomed on either side
Nor has any dove of peace flown across

→

सितम तो ये है कि दोनों को वहम है कि बहार
अदू के खून में नहाने के बाद आती है
तुम्हें यह ज़ोम महाभारत लड़ी तुमने
हमें यह फ़ख़र कि हम करबला के आदी हैं
ये हुआ है हाल इस ज़िंदगी का कि अब
तुम्हारे पांव सलामत रहे न हाथ ही मेरे
हमारे शहरों की मजबूर बेनवा मख़लूक
दबी हुई दुखों के हज़ार ढेरों में
अब उनकी तीरा-नसीबी चराग़ चाहती है
तुम्हारे शहर में आया हूं दोस्तो, अबके
न शे'रो नग़मों की महफिल न शायरी के लिये
अगर तुम्हारी अना का सवाल है तो फिर
चलो मैं हाथ बढ़ाता हूं दोस्ती के लिये

Sitam to ye hai ki dono ko veham hai ki bahaar
Adu ke khoon mein nahane ke baad aati hai
Tumhen yeh zom mahabharat lari tumne
Humein yeh fakhar ki hum karbala ke aadi hein
Ye hua hai haal is zindagi ka ki ab
Tumhare paon salamat rahe na hath hi mere
Humare shehron ki majboor benava makhluk
Dabi hui dukhon ke hazar dheron mein
Ab unki teera-nasibi charag chahati hai
Tumhare shehar mein aaya hoon dosto abke
Na shero nagmon ki mehfil na shayari ke liye
Agar tumhari ana ka sawal hai to phir
Chalo main hath badhata hun dosti ke liye

And the cruel cut is that both of us think
That the spring comes after bathing in enemy's blood;
You are proud of the fact that you fought Mahabharata
And we are proud that we are used to the rigours
of Karbala;
Now things have come to such a pass
That neither my hands are mine nor your feet your
own;
O now the hapless; voiceless masses of each country
Buried, as they are, under a pile of misery—
Their dark lives demand light.
This time I have come to your city
Not for poetry, nor for any symposium
But on a mission of amity
And if in this, it is your ego that stands in the way
Here I am extending my hand of friendship
Take it, pray.

हम अपने ख़्वाब क्यों बेचें

फ़क़ीराना रविश[1] रखते हैं
लेकिन इस क़दर नादार[2] हम कब थे
कि अपने ख़्वाब बेचें

हम अपने ज़ख़्म आँखों में लिए फिरते थे
लेकिन रौनक़े-बाज़ार[3] हम कब थे
हमारे हाथ ख़ाली थे
मगर ऐसा न था फिर भी
कि हम अपनी दरीदा-दामनी[4]
और जाने-शोरीदा[5] लिए
गलियों में आवाज़ लगाते
'ख़्वाब ले लो, ख़्वाब लोगो!'

→

Faqirana ravish rakhte hain
Lekin is qadar nadaar hum kab the
Ki apne khwab bechen

Hum apne zakhm aankhon mein liye phirte the
Lekin raunke-bazar hum kab the
Humare hath khali the
Magar aisa na tha phir bhi
Ki hum apni darida-damani
Aur jaane-shorida liye
Galiyon mein awaz lagate
'Khwab le lo, khwab logo !'

---

1. साधु-संतों सा व्यवहार 2. दरिद्र 3. बाज़ार के लायक़ 4. जर्जर दामन 5. जीर्ण जिस्म

Why should we sell our dreams

True, we are simple-minded people
But we are not such paupers
That we would sell our dreams.

We went about with our wounds visible in our eyes
But we were never a show-piece for the market,
We were empty handed with tattered dress on our battered body
But that doesn't mean, we would be hawking our dreams through the streets,

→

इतने कम पिंदार[1] हम कब थे
हम अपने ख़्वाब क्यों बेचें
कि जिनको देखने की आरज़ू[2] में
हमने आँखें तक गँवा दीं
और आशिक़ी में
और हवाख़्वाही[3] में
हर तरग़ीब[4] की शम्एँ बुझा दीं

चलो हम बेनवा
महरूमे-सक़फ़ो-बामो-दर[5] ठहरे
चलो हम बदमुक़द्दर[6], बेहुनर ठहरे

→

Itne kam pindar hum kab the
Hum apne khwab kyon bechen
Ki jinko dekhne ki aarzoo mein
Humne aankhen tak ganva di
Aur aashiqi mein
Aur hawakhwahi mein
Her targeeb ki shammaen bujha din

Chalo hum benava
Mehrume-sakapho-bamo-dar thehre
Chalo hum badmukaddar, be-hunar thehre

1. अहंवादी 2. इच्छा 3. हवाख़ोरी 4. प्रलोभन 5. छत, द्वार से वंचित 6. बुरा भाग्य

We were never so scant of self-respect
That we would sell our dreams
To see which we lost our eyes
And for the sake of which
We extinguished every other desire.

Granted, we have no voice, no roof
over our head
No fortune and no skill

→

पर अपने आस्माँ की दास्तानें
और ज़मीं के अंजमो-महताब[1] क्यों बेचें
ख़रीदारो!
तुम अपने काग़ज़ी अंबार लाए हो
हवस की मंडियों से दिरहमो-दीनार[2] लाए हो
तुम ऐसे दाम तो हर बार लाए हो
मगर तुम पर
हम अपने हर्फ़ के ताऊस[3]
अपने ख़ून के सुर्ख़ाब क्यों बेचें

Per apne aasmaan ki dastanen
Aur zamin ke anjumo-mehtab kyon bechen
Kharidaro !
Tum apne kagzi ambaar laye ho
Havas ki mandiyon se dirhamo-dinar laye ho
Tum aise daam to har baar laye ho
Magar tum per
Hum apne hurf ke taaus
Apne khoon ke surkhab kyon bechen

1. चाँद-तारे 2. मुद्राएँ 3. सिंहासन

But why should we sell the legends of our glory and
the glow of our earth
O buyers,
You, who have brought wads of currency notes
And bags full of gold coins from the bazaars of
lust,
This price you have always offered
But why should we sell
The wealth of our words,
Our priceless self-respect
In exchange for this!

ख़्वाब मरते नहीं

ख़्वाब मरते नहीं
ख़्वाब दिल है न आँखें न साँसें कि जो
रेज़ा-रेज़ा हुए तो बिखर जाएंगे
जिस्म की मौत से ये भी मर जाएंगे
ख़्वाब मरते नहीं
ख़्वाब तो रौशनी हैं, नवा[1] हैं, हवा हैं
जो काले पहाड़ों से रुकते नहीं
ज़ुल्म के दोज़खों से भी फुंकते नहीं
रौशनी और नवा और हवा के अलम[2]
मक़तलों में पहुंच कर भी झुकते नहीं
ख़्वाब तो हर्फ़ हैं
ख़्वाब तो नूर[3] हैं
ख़्वाब सुक़रात हैं
ख़्वाब मन्सूर हैं

Khwab marte nahin
Khwab dil hai na aankhen na saansen ki jo
Reza-reza hue to bikhar jayenge
Jism ki maut se ye bhi mar jayenge
Khwab marte nahin
Khwab to raushani hain, nava hain, hawa hain
Jo kale paharon se rukte nahin
Zulm ke dozakhon se bhi phukte nahin
Raushani aur nava aur hawa ke alam
Maqtalon mein pahunch kar bhi jhukte nahin
Khwab to hurf hain
Khwab to noor hain
Khwab suqrat hain
Khwab mansoor hain

---

1. आवाज 2. झंडा 3. रोशनी, प्रकाश

Dreams never die

Dreams never die.
Dreams are not eyes, heart or breath
Which will be scattered, if broken
Or die with the death of the body.
Dreams are light, dreams are a voice, dreams are wind
Which cannot be stopped by dark mountains
Which even the tyranny's hell-fires cannot burn.
The flags of light, voice and wind
Even when taken to the slaughter house do not bend
Dreams are words
Dreams are light
Dreams are Socrates, dreams are Mansoor—
Emblems of truth and might,
Dreams never die.

गाओ

गाओ कि मुझे यक़ीं नहीं है
तुम अबके गए तो आ सकोगे
दहलीज़ से एक क़दम उतर कर
वो राहगुज़ार मुन्तज़िर[1] है
जिस पर जो कोई चला गया है
क़दमों के निशाँ बिछा गया है
फ़ुरक़त[2] के दीये जला गया है।

Gao ki mujhe yaqin nahin hai
Tum abke gaye to aa sakoge
Dehleez se ek qadam utar kar
Woh raahguzaar muntzir hai
Jis per jo koi chala gaya hai
Qadmon ke nishan bichha gaya hai
Furqat ke diye jala gaya hai

---

1. प्रतीक्षारत 2. वियोग

Sing

Sing, because I am not sure
That this time if you go
You will ever come back;
For, anybody who has left this threshold
And gone on the road, lying ahead,
Has only left his footprints behind,
Has lit only candles of eternal wait.

और तेरे शहर से

और तेरे शहर से जब रुख़सते-सफर बांध लिया
दरो-दीवार पे हसरत की नज़र क्या करते
चांद कुम्हली हुई शाम की दहलीज़ पे था
उस घड़ी तेरे मजबूरे-सफ़र क्या करते
दिल ठहर जाने को कहता था, मगर क्या करते

हमने जब वादी-ए-गुरबत[1] में क़दम रखा था
जिस तरह यादे-वतन आती थी समझाने को
कुछ उस तरह की कैफ़ियतें जो आज भी हैं
जिस तरह कोई क़यामत हो गुज़र जाने को
जिस तरह कोई फिर कहे पलट आने को

Aur tere shehar se jab rukhsate-safar bandh liya
Daro-dewar pe hasrat ki nazar kya karte
Chand kumhali hui shaam ki dehleez pe tha
Us ghari tere majbure-safar kya karte
Dil thehar jaane ko kehta tha, magar kya karte

Humne jab vadi-e-gurbat mein qadam rakha tha
Jis tarah yade-vatan aati thi samjhane ko
Kuchh us tarah ki qaifiyate jo aaj bhi hain
Jis tarah koi qayamat ho guzar jaane ko
Jis tarah koi phir kahe palat aane ko

---

1. परदेस

And from your city

Since I had decided to leave your city
There was no use casting a wistful eye
The moon was shining dimly on the threshold of
the evening
And I felt a strong urge to stay on,
But I had no alternative but to leave

Like the memories of my city which haunted me
When I first stepped into the valley of my exile
Quite similar to that is my state of mind now;
Even now, I feel as I felt when I was in that alien city
As if I were facing the day of judgement
Even now somebody seems to be urging me to
come back.

चांद रुकता है न...

चांद रुकता है न आती है सबा में ज़िंदानों[1] के पास
कौन ले जाये मेरे नामे[2] मेरे जानां के पास
अब बजुज़[3] तरके-वफ़ा कोई खयाल आता नहीं
अब कोई हीला नहीं शायद दिले-नादां के पास
चन्द यादें नोहागर[4] हैं खेमा-ए-दिल के करीब
चन्द तस्वीरें भटकती हैं सफ़े-मिज़गां[5] के पास
शहर वाले सब अमीरे-शहर की मजलिस में हैं
कौन आयेगा ग़रीबे-शहरे नापुरसां के पास

Chand rukta hai na aati hai seba zindano ke paas
Kaun le jaaye mere naame merey jaanan ke paas
Ab bajuz tarke-wafa koi khyal aata nahin
Ab koi hiila nahin shayad dile-nadan ke paas
Chand yaaden nohagar hain khema-e-dil ke qareeb
Chand tasveerein bhatakti hain saphe-mizgaan ke paas
Shehar wale sab ameere-shehar ki majlis mein hai
Kaun aayega garibe-shehre napursa ke paas

---

1. जेलखाना 2. पत्र 3. सिवा 4. रो रही है 5. पलकों

Neither the moon stops by...

Neither the moon stops by nor the breeze visits the prison house
Who'll take my missive to my beloved !
No other thought except to give up loving crosses my mind,
My poor heart has no alternative left now.
A few memories are moving around in the vicinity of the ruined heart,
A few pictures float about the desolate eyes,
The townsmen have all gone over to the chief's side
Who will from that heartless place visit me in exile.

नई मुसाफ़त[1] का अहदनामा[2]

मेरा लहू रायगाँ[3] नहीं था
जो मेरे दीवारो-दर से टपका
तो शाहराहों तक आ गया था
जहाँ किसी को गुमाँ[4] नहीं था
मेरा लहू राएगाँ नहीं था
मेरे मुक़द्दर में आबरू
की तमाम लंबी मुसाफ़तें थीं
मेरे सफ़र में
हुसैन के सर मसीह के जिस्म
की सभी दर्दनाकियाँ थीं, अज़ीयतें[5] थीं

→

Mera lahu rayegan nahin tha
jo mere dewaro-dar se tapka
to shahrahon tak aa gaya tha
jahan kisee ko guman nahin tha
mera lahu rayegan nahin tha
mere muqaddar mein aabaru
ki tamam lambi musafaten thin
mere safar mein
Hussain ke sar masih ke jism
ki sabhi dardnakiyan thin, aziyaten thin

---

1. सफर 2. अनुबंध पत्र 3. व्यर्थ 4. भ्रम 5. यंत्रणाएँ

The Contract of a new journey

My blood is not so cheap,
That dripping from my home and hearth,
It would flow on to the thoroughfare
Where nobody would notice it;
My blood won't be wasted like this.
Long journeys were in store for me;
My journey entailed agony and pain
Of christ and Hussain

→

मगर मेरा दर्द बे-वक़र[1] था
मगर मेरा दश्त[2] बे-शजर[3] था
ये बात बरसों की है, तो हो
पर वो साअतें अब भी नौहागर[4] हैं
जहाँ कहीं भी हुजूम होता
तो सब मेरी सम्त[5] देखते
और तन्ज़[6] करते
कि उसको देखो
ये कौन पैकर[7] है
जिसका चेहरा नहीं

Magar mera dard be-vaqar tha
Magar mera dasht be-shajar tha
Ye baat barson ki hai, to ho
Per woh saaeten ab bhi nauhagar hain
Jahan kahin bhi hujoom hota
To sab meri samt dekhte
Aur tanz karte
Ki usko dekho
Ye kaun paikar hai
Jiska chehra nahin

1. तुच्छ 2. जंगल 3. पेड़ों से रहित 4. शोक-गीत गा रही हैं 5. ओर 6. कटाक्ष 7. आकृति

My journeys were, however, minor,
But the forests on my way were gray.
What if it happened ages ago,
Those occasions are till painfully around
The crowds would look at me
And sardonically say :
Look at that shape,
It has no face.

दुश्मन का क़सीदा

हम कि तलवार के दुश्मन थे
कि तलवार अदू थी अपनी
अब मदह-ख़्वां[1] हैं
कि तलवार का किरदार[2] भी था
और हरीफ़[3] अपना
कोई यारे-जिगरदार भी था
और वो यारे-जिगरदार तरहदार[4] भी था।
न कि बारूद की नाली
न कि फ़ौलाद का ख़ोल

न कि बुज़दिल का मुअक्क़फ़[5]
न कि कमज़र्फ़ का बोल
कि हमेशा रही तलवार
किसी हर्फ़े-सफ़ा[6] की मानिंद
सच के परचम की तरह
दिल की सदा की मानिंद
न कि मुल्ला की क़बा और रिया[7] की मानिंद
न मुनाफ़िक़[8] की दुआ की मानिंद

Hum ki talwar ke dushman the
Ki talwar adu thi apni
Ab madah-khwan hain
Ki talwar ka kirdar bhi tha
Aur hareef apna
Koi yare-jigardar bhi tha
Aur woh yare-jigardar tarahdar bhi tha
Na ki barood ki naali
Na ki faulad ka khol

Na ki buzdil ka moakif
Na ki kamzarf ka bol
Ki hamesha rahi talwar
Kisee hurfe-safa ki manind
Sach ke percham ki tarah
Dil ki sada ki manind
Na ki mullah ki qaba aur riya ki manind
Na munafiq ki dua ki manind

---

1. प्रशंसक 2. चरित्र 3. दुश्मन प्रतिद्वंद्वी 4. शोख़ तबीयत रखने वाला 5. विचार-राय, 6. पवित्र शब्द 7. झूठ 8. पाखंडी

Eulogy to the Enemy

I, who was an enemy of the sword once
Or the sword was whose enemy,
Am its great admirer now,
Because the sword had a character
And my rival had a heart
And was a colourful person.
He was not merely a barrel of the gun
Or a sheath
Or the argument of a coward
Or the utterance of the mean.
The sword was always like a sacred word.
The banner of truth,
Like the voice of the heart
Rather than the falsehood and the apparel of
the mullah
Or the hypocrite's prayer, never.

इतने चुप क्यों हो

इतने चुप क्यों हो रफ़ीकाने-सफ़र[1], कुछ तो कहो
दर्द से चूर हुए हो, कि क़रार आया है
भर गया हिज्र का हर ज़ख्म कि जी हार चले
बुझ गया शौक़ कि पैग़ाम-निगार आया है
नामुरादी[2] की थकन है कि खुमारे-शबे-वस्ल
जाँ सुलगती है कि चेहरे पे निखार आया है

कितनी उजड़ी हुई रुत है कि सुकूं है न जुनूं
इतनी बेकैफ़[3] हुई बादे-बहारी[4] कैसे
न कहीं नोहा-ए-जाँ है न कहीं नग़मा-ए-दिल
कुछ तो बोलो कि शबे-दर्द गुज़ारी कैसे
बाज़ी-ए-राहे-तलब[5] जीत के हारी कैसे

Itne chup kyon ho rafiqane-safar, kuchh to kaho
Dard se choor hue ho, ki qaraar aaya hai
Bhar gaya hijra ka her zakhm ki ji haar chale
Bujh gaya shauq ki paigaam-nigaar aaya hai
Namuradi ki thakan hai ki khumare-shabe-vasl
Jaan sulagti hai ki chehre pe nikhar aaya hai

Kitni ujri hui rut hai sukun hai na junoon
Itni bekaif hui bade-vahari kaise
Na kahin noha-e-jaan hai na kahin nagma-e-dil
Kuchh to bolo ki shabe-dard guzaari kaise
Baazi-e-rahe-talab jeet ke haari kaise

---

1. सफ़र के साथी 2. असफलता 3. बेमज़ा 4. वसंत की हवा 5. आरज़ू की बाज़ी

Why are you so quiet

Why are you so quiet, O my fellow-traveller?
Are you suffocated with pain or feeling relieved,
Feeling fulfilled or have you lost heart,
Are you done with your passion or is it its helm,
Is it a fatigue of failure or ecstacy of union,
Or, is it a case of a face flushed with glow;

Or, is it that your heart burns ?
O how desolate! neither is this peace, nor passion
So lacklustre is the spring
That there is neither lamentation of death
Nor celebration of love!
Tell us, pray, how you passed the night of pain
And how the game, you had won, you lost again!

पास क्या था

पास क्या था कि लूटती दुनिया
हम तो कल भी थे बेसरो-सामां[1]

आज दीवार खिंच गयी है अगर
शहर कल भी था सूरते ज़िंदां[2]

कब मयस्सर हुआ था रोज़े-विसाल[3]
कब मुक़द्दर न था शबे-हिज्रां[4]

इक मताए-सुखन[5] थी पास अपने
एक साज़े-वफ़ा था दौलते जां

दर्द क़ायम है, याद बाकी है
इक तेरी दीद छिन गयी जानां

Pass kya tha ki looti duniya
Hum to kal bhi the besaro-samaan

Aaj dewar khinch gayee hai agar
Shehar kal bhi tha surate zindan

Kab mayassar hua tha roze-visaal
Kab muqaddar ne tha shabe-hijran

Ik matae-sukhan thi pass apne
Ek saaze-wafa tha daulate jaan

Dard qayam hai, yaad baaki hai
Ik teri deed chhin gayee jaanan

1. निर्धन 2. जेल की तरह 3. मिलन का दिन 4. वियोग की रात 5. शायरी की दौलत

What did I have

What did I have which the world could rob me of
I was a destitute earlier too

Today, though I am behind bars
The world, outside also wasn't better than a prison house

Which day was a day of union
Which night was not a night of separation

Only my poems were my assets
My loyalty was all my wealth

The anguish is still there, the memory remains
Only, I have been deprived of your sight, my love

पिछला पहर

न कहीं शहरे-मेहरबां की हवा
न कोई यारे-हमदमो-दमसाज़
न सरे-बाम[1] ज़ुल्फे-आवारा
न सरे-राह चश्मे-फ़ितनासाज़[2]
न कहीं कूए-चाक दामाना
न कोई रुए-दोस्ताने फ़राज़
न कोई बैते-बेदिलो-ग़ालिब[3]
न कोई शेरे हाफिज़ो-शीराज़
न कोई शम्मे कुश्ता-शबे[4] है
न कोई अंदलीबे-सीनागुदाज़[5]

→

Na kaheen shehare-meharban ki hava
Na koi yaare-humdamo-damsaaz
Na sare-baam zulfe-awara
Na sare-raah chashme-fitnasaaz
Na kahin kue-chaak damaana
Na koi rue-dostane Faraz
Na koi bait-e-Bedilo-Ghalib
Na koi shere Hafiz-o-Shiraaz
Na koi shamme kushta-shabe hai
Na koi andlibe-sina gudaaz

---

1. छत पर 2. दिलकश नज़र 3. ग़ालिब और बेदिल का शे'र 4. रात की मारी हुई 5. दिल को छूने वाला बुलबुल का गीत

The last hour of night

Neither the breeze from the friendly city
Nor a pal or confidante,
Neither the beloved dear with bewitching eyes
Nor her lovely lock from the terrace, floating,
Neither a passionate kindred soul
Nor anyone close to my heart,
Neither a couplet from Ghalib or Bedil
Nor a verse from Hafiz and Sheeraz,
Neither a night-consumed candle
Nor the nightingale's heart-rending song.

→

ख़िलवते[1]-गम, न बज़्मे-रुसवाई
न सवाले-तबलो अर्ज़े-नियाज़
चार-सू इक फ़सील बेदर है
चार जानिब हिसारे[2]-बेअंदाज़
ऐसी वीरानियों से घबराकर
जब उठाता हूँ तेरी याद का साज़
तोड़ देती है सिलसिले सारे
पहरेदारों की बदनुमा आवाज़

Khilwate-ghum, na bazme-ruswai
Na sawale-tablo arze-niyaaz
Chaar-su ik faseel bedar hai
Chaar janib hisare-beandaaz
Aisee veeraniyon se ghabrakar
Jab uthata hun teri yaad ka saaz
Tor deti hai silsile saare
Pehredari ki badnuma awaaz

---

1. तन्हाई 2. घेरा

Neither the peace of solitude nor company whatever,
Surrounded by a wall without an exit
With sleep having left my eyes—
In this state, desolate and forelorn
When I pick up the lyre of your memories
My reverie is broken
By the harsh and grating voice of the prison guards

क़ातिल

क़ातिल चुप है
खूँ-आलूदा[1] हाथ में अब तक
खंजर थर-थर काँप रहा है
लोगों का अंबोह[2] उसे
घेरे में लेकर, चीख़ रहा है
ये क़ातिल है
ये क़ातिल है

ख़ाक़ और खूँ में लथपथ लाश
के होटों पर
इक बात जमी है

→

Qatil chup hai
Khoon-aaluda hath mein ab tak
Khanjar thar-thar kaanp raha hai
Logon ka amboh use
Ghere mein lekar, cheekh raha hai
Ye qatil hai
Ye qatil hai

Khaaq aur khoon mein lathpath laash
Ke hoton per
Ik baat jami hai

---

1. ख़ून में सने हाथ 2. भीड़

Murderer

The murderer is silent
His blood-stained hand
Holding the sword
Is trembling still ;
A crowd of people
Has surrounded him and is shouting
He is a murderer, he is a murderer.

The dead body, besmeared in blood and dust
Loudly proclaims

→

ये क़ातिल है
लेकिन किसका
ये अपनी तख़लीक़[1] *का क़ातिल*
इसने ख़ुद को क़त्ल किया है
लोगों का अंबोह मगर
कब सुनता है
कौन है क़ातिल
किसने
किसको क़त्ल किया है

Ye qatil hai
Lekin kiska
Ye apni takhleeq ka qatil
Isne khud ko qatal kiya hai
Logon ka amboh magar
Kab sunta hai
Kaun hai qatil
Kisne
Kisko qatal kiya hai

---

1. रचना

He is a murderer but he has murdered his own
creation,

He has murdered himself.
But the crowd keeps shouting
Who is the murdered,
Whom has he murdered!

कोई भटकता बादल

दूर इक शहर से जब कोई भटकता बादल
मेरी जलती हुई बस्ती की तरफ आयेगा
कितनी हसरत से उसे देखेंगी प्यासी आंखें
और वो वक्त की मानिंद गुज़र जायेगा।

जाने किस सोच में खो जायेगी दिल की दुनिया
जाने क्या-क्या मुझे बीता हुआ याद आयेगा
और उस शहर का बेफैज़[1] भटकता बादल
दर्द की आग को फैला के चला जायेगा

Door ik shehar se jab koi bhatakta badal
Meri jalti hui basti ki taraf aayega
Kitni hasrat se use dekhengi pyasi aankhen
Aur woh waqt ki manind guzar jaayega

Jaane kis soch mein kho jaayegi dil ki duniya
Jaane kya-kya mujhe beeta hua yaad aayega
Aur us shehar ki befaiz bhatakta badal
Dard ki aag ko phaila ke chala jaayega

---

1. कंजूस

A wandering cloud

When a cloud from a distant city
Comes hovering over my burning town
Most wistfully would I be looking at it ;
But like the time flying, it would soon flit away.

My heart would be drowned in strange thoughts
And I would remember the times past
But the unkind cloud from that city
Would only kindle the fire of anguish
And pass by

सच भी झूटा है

सच भी झूटा है
कि इसके भी कई चेहरे हैं
एक चेहरा कि तेरे क़ुर्ब की साअत[1] में मुझे
न कोई ख़्वाहिशे-आग़ोश[2]-रसी[3]
और न तमन्ना-ए-विसाल
एक चेहरा कि
तिरे जिस्म की हुरमत[4] की क़सम खा के
हर इक दीदा-ए-मश्कूक[5] को समझाता रहा
आसमानों के सहीफ़ों[6] से उतारे हुए
अलफ़ाज़ को दोहराता रहा

→

Sach bhi jhoota hai
Ki iske bhi kai chehre hain
Ek chehra ki tere qurb ki saaet mein mujhe
Na koi khwahishe-aagosh-rasi
Aur na tamanna-e-visaal
Ek chehra ki
Tere jism ki hurmat ki Qasam kha ke
Her ik deeda-e-mashkook ko samjhata raha
Aasmanon ke sahifon se utare hue
Alfaz ko dohrata raha

---

1. क्षण 2. गोद की ख़्वाहिश 3. पहुंच 4. प्रतिष्ठा 5. संदिग्ध 6. धर्मग्रंथ-पुस्तक

Truth is also a lie

Truth is also a lie
It has many faces :
A face, when I am with you
And have neither the desire for closer proximity
Nor for the warmth of your lap;
A face, which swore by the dignity of your body,
Understood every suspicious eye
And recited from the holy book
Descended from the sky;

→

एक चेहरा
कि तेरे पास से उठा हूँ
तो खुद सोचता हूँ
कि मेरा सर्द लहू
गर्मी-ए-शौक़ से और आतिशे-महरूमी[1] से
क्यों फुंकता है
और बदन
नशे के आलम में भी क्यों दुःखता है।

Ek chehra
Ki tere pass se utha hun
To khud sochta hun
Ki mera sard lahu
Garmi-e-shauq se aur aatishe-mehrumi se,
Kyon phunkta hai
Aur badan
Nashe ke aalam mein bhi kyon dukhta hai

1. निराशा की आग

Another face,
when I get up from your side
And wonder
Why the cold blood burns with the heat of passion
and the scolding of deprivation
And the body aches even in the state of inebriation

ख़्वाब

वो चाँद मेरा हमसफ़र था
दूरी के उजाड़ जंगलों में
अब मेरी नज़र से छुप चुका है

एक उम्र से मैं मलूलो-तन्हा[1]
ज़ुल्मात[2] की रहगुज़र[3] में हूँ
मैं आगे बढ़ूं कि लौट आऊं

क्या सोच के इन्तज़ार में हूँ
कोई भी नहीं जो ये बताये
मैं कौन हूँ किस दयार[4] में हूँ

Woh chand mera hamsafar tha
Doori ke ujaar jangalon mein
Ab meri nazar se chhup chuka hai

Ek umra se main malul-o-tanha
Zulmaat ki rehguzar mein hun
Main aage badhun ki laut aaun

Kya soch ke intzaar mein hun
Koi bhi nahin jo ye bataye
Main kaun hun kis dayaar mein hun

1. उदास 2. अंधेरे 3. गली 4. शहर

Dreams

The moon that was my fellow-traveller
In the wasteland of the far-off forests
Is hidden from my sight

For a long time now
In the dark pathways of life
Lonely and sad
I cannot decide
Whether to go back or forge further ahead ;

I don't know who I am waiting for
For, there is none who can tell me
Who I am, and where !

यह तब की बात है

मैंने कहा था
दिल के सफ़र में
यूँ तो बहुत सी मंज़िलें हैं
लेकिन
जानाँ[1]
तुमसे आगे कोई नहीं
आज मगर मजबूरे-सफ़र[2] *हूँ*

Maine kaha tha
dil ke safar mein
yoon to bahut see manzilen hain
lekin
jaanan
tumse aage koi nahin
aaj magar majbure-safar hoon

---

1. महबूब 2. लाचारी में यात्रा

It was then

It was then
That I had said :
In the journey of the heart
There is many a destination
But none beyond you
But, my love, it was then
Today, I must move on.

नोहा

अगर्चे मरगे-वफ़ा[1] भी इक
साहिना[2] है लेकिन बेहिसी
इससे भी बढ़के जानकाह[3] है
कि जब ख़ुद हम अपने हाथों
अपनी चाहत को नामुरादी
को रेगज़ारों[4] में दफ़न करके
जुदा हुए तो
न तेरी पलकों पे कोई आंसू
लरज़ रहा था, न मेरे होंठों
पे कोई जाँ-सोज़ मरसिया[5] था

Agarche marge-wafa bhi ik
sahina hai lekin behisi
isse bhi badhke jaankaah
ki jab khud hum apne haathon
apni chahat ko namuradi
ko regzaron mein dafan karke
juda hue to
na teri palkon pe koi aansu
laraj raha tha, na mere hoton
pe koi jaan-soze marsiya tha

---

1. प्रेम की मौत 2. त्रासदी 3. जानलेवा 4. रेगिस्तानों 5. मृत्यु-गीत

Elegy

Although the death of true love is a tragedy
Indifference is more painful and worse;
So when after burying our luckless love in the desert
sands
We parted
There was neither a tear moistening your eye
Nor was there a sad word on my lips
Mourning the demise of love

❑❑❑